SIMULATION AND NATIONAL DEVELOPMENT

SIMULATION
AND
NATIONAL
DEVELOPMENT

ANDREW M. SCOTT

WITH WILLIAM A. LUCAS AND TRUDI M. LUCAS

Department of Political Science
University of North Carolina
Chapel Hill, North Carolina

JOHN WILEY & SONS, INC.   NEW YORK   LONDON   SYDNEY

PREFACE

The authors' interest in simulation derived originally from a reading of *Simulation in International Relations** by Harold Guetzkow and his associates at Northwestern University. Our first simulation effort was a replication of an inter-nation exercise described in that volume. Before long, we began to wonder if the relations of actors *within* a society could not be simulated in much the same way that relations between nations were being done. We decided it was possible, and undertook to simulate political conditions in a developing nation.

A series of intra-nation simulations were developed, as well as one dealing with an urban community. Our book describes these experiments in gaming, assesses the strengths and weaknesses of each, and discusses the usefulness of simulation in the study of political and other processes. Chapters 2, 4, 6, and 8 are abstracts of game packets distributed to the players for each game. Generous portions of the scenarios for these games are included to convey a sense of what the game was like, and to illustrate the aids and techniques that were developed for use in each game. The description of the Chilean exercise is skeletal, however, since, in important respects, the game was similar to the Brazilian simulation.

Chapter 7 discusses simulation of the political processes of Durham, North Carolina, and Chapter 8 presents the scenario of the Durham game. While the city selected for the experiment was an American city, the technique has obvious application to towns and cities in the

---

**Simulation in International Relations: Developments for Research and Teaching*. Harold Guetzkow, Chadwick F. Alger, Richard A. Brody, Robert C. Noel, Richard C. Snyder (Englewood Cliffs, New Jersey: Prentice-Hall, 1963).

developing countries. If one city can be simulated, so can another. In addition, we were eager to demonstrate that simulation could be applied to the study of social change in cities. If simulation has as broad an application to social situations as we believe, then it should be applicable to cities as well as to nations and, indeed, to almost any social system.

By tracing the evolution of our thinking from game to game, we hope to avoid taking too much for granted. Over a period of time, and as a consequence of growing familiarity with the problems of simulation, it becomes easy to take for granted things that are not at all self-evident to others. Thinking continues to be influenced by the insights that have passed from the explicit to the implicit level, without the experimenters being fully aware of how much they are taking for granted. A chronological treatment eases the task of making the implicit explicit. The analysis that will be offered, and the scenarios that are included, may prove helpful to others interested in replicating these exercises or in trying to move beyond the present work.

In the last chapter, we discuss the theory and methodology of simulation, its usefulness as a teaching device, as an aid to policy making, and for research and theory building. Our conclusions about the potential of simulation are not based solely on the types of games developed at the University of North Carolina.

The exercises described here were designed to reproduce situations encountered by actors in the social systems under study. A strong point of these games has proved to be their capacity to enhance a player's grasp of political and social realities. If a simulate of a field situation is to be realistic, it must reproduce with some fidelity the complexity of that situation. When this complexity is reproduced, however, so many variables must be incorporated that the experimenter will not be able to maintain close control over them. Simulation of a complex field situation, therefore, is quite different from an experiment, conducted under laboratory conditions, in which all but one or two variables are controlled. If this difference is held in mind, a good deal of confusion about what can and cannot be done with the type of simulation described in this book will be avoided.

In our work, we received important and extensive help from Professor Robert Daland of the University of North Carolina. We also received assistance from Ricardo Tichauer, Anne Murphy, Charles Cnudde, Eleanor Main, Kenneth Sherrill, and others, also of the University of North Carolina. Mrs. Geraldine Foster provided valuable editorial assistance. We would like to thank the School of Public

Health at the University of North Carolina for a grant relating to the use of simulation as a training technique, and to the administrators of a Peace Corps training project for defraying the costs of the Brazilian exercise that made use of Peace Corps trainees. The senior author would also like to thank the Faculty Research Council of the University of North Carolina for a grant supporting his work in this field.

Andrew M. Scott
William A. Lucas
Trudi M. Lucas

Chapel Hill, North Carolina
February, 1966

CONTENTS

1

SIMULAND: SIMULATION OF A HYPOTHETICAL DEVELOPING NATION

With over three decades still remaining, the twentieth century has already broken all records for change. Prior to World War II, change went on primarily in the developed areas of the world. Since the war, however, virtually the entire world has been shaken and shaped by revolutionary upheaval. Areas once isolated, or slumbering under colonial rule as late as the 1940's, have, in quick succession, gained political independence, and fallen heir to the scores of problems associated with economic, social, and political development. The study of change in these developing areas is a task of first importance, one to which scholars have responded readily. Anthropologists, sociologists, psychologists, economists, political scientists, and others, have responded, not merely because the problem is important—there are many important problems that receive no serious attention—but because it is so complex, so intellectually stimulating, and admits of optimism about an ultimate solution.

It occurred to us, in the fall of 1964, that simulation might prove useful in the study of the developing areas. If an observer could simplify the complexity of development, and compress the time required for its evolution, might he not be able to learn about the larger process by studying the miniature? Might not simulation provide the observer with a tool for penetrating and grasping a process that would

1

otherwise seem hopelessly complex? When a new investigative tool such as simulation is developed, a number of years may elapse before it comes to be applied to the full range of problems that could benefit from it. Simulation, in a sense, is a solution looking for a problem. The study of developing areas, on the other hand, represents a problem looking for a solution. We decided to join the problem and the new investigative technique in what we hoped would be a marriage both pragmatic and congenial.

Intrigued by the idea that simulation might provide a useful training tool and an instrument for studying the processes of development, we invented, in the Spring of 1964, the country of Simuland.

Simuland was given a number of features that would be typical of developing countries. It was organized on the basis of seven competing elites: the landed gentry; the entrepreneurial elite; the intelligentsia and the students; the bureaucracy; the Communist Party; military branch A; and military branch B.

We constructed the game so that activity centered around the government. The government was to focus its attention on aiding economic development and staying in power. The power base of the government of Simuland was a coalition of elite elements; only so long as the President could hold his coalition intact could he remain in office. If the government failed to satisfy critically important elite demands, a number of elite elements could form an opposition coalition and force the government out of office. Because the bureaucracy was allowed to pursue its own interests, it had a degree of autonomy; however, it could never directly disobey the President.

The game was structured so that the government was headed by a member of the landed gentry, and supported by the more conservative of the two military factions in the country. Despite the nature of his allies, the President had to work at stimulating economic growth in the country lest he alienate all the other elite elements. As built into the game, the growth rate of the economy was a function of total investment, both public and private. To achieve maximum growth, the President had to increase taxes and reduce funds allocated to the military; he also had to persuade the elites controlling the economic *status quo* to reduce consumption and increase investment. The game thus centered around the inherent conflict between the government's need to stimulate economic growth and its need to maintain political support.

The masses of Simuland were passive. They could take no initiative and could only react to initiatives undertaken by the elites. Their part was played by the experimenters, who estimated the success that a given initiative might have with the masses, and translated this estimate into increased or decreased support for the elite involved. The experimenters also reported on the country's economic growth and on the profits for individual elites. Both public opinion changes and economic changes had a direct impact upon the basic strengths of the elite elements and the government. These strengths were expressed quantitatively, and became salient factors in inter-elite negotiations. The position of one elite in the eyes of the other elites was, therefore, affected by two factors: first, its direct interaction with those elites, and, second, the feedback on that elite contributed by the experimenters.

We felt that a model of a developing society which treats that society as an isolate introduces a significant distortion. Developing societies are not isolates set apart from their environment. If they were, they would probably not be developing. Indeed, external influences—other nations and international organizations—are likely to be extremely influential in shaping the developmental patterns of a nation. Therefore, built into the game was a foreign environment consisting of three countries, all played by the experimenters. The experimenters decided on requests for foreign aid addressed to these countries, and attached such political strings to the aid as seemed realistic.

The game was constructed so that the elites in Simuland would act, for the most part, in a unified manner. A player who was a member of a particular elite was supposed to act in accordance with the interests of that elite, as he understood them. The interests of each elite were given for the elite as a whole, and different viewpoints and variant interests were not prescribed for individual players. In keeping with the assignment of interests to elites as wholes, the three players in each elite were assigned to one room, and major decisions were taken in a way that did not permit one player to veto the wishes of the other two.

Communications arrangements are often extremely important in a simulation exercise. In Simuland, they included a newspaper, written communication (via non-playing messengers), and word of mouth. The President and members of the bureaucracy had free physical movement and could communicate orally with any player. However, a member of an elite had to petition the experimenters for permission to have oral conference with a member of another elite; and only one member of an elite at a time could meet with a representative of another elite. This rule, like most of the other rules, was established in the interest of versimilitude. An elite in a country does not, in fact, meet as a unit with another elite.

To enable the experimenters to reconstruct the activity of the game after it was played, we supplemented the written record of messages and agreements among the players with a running account prepared by a roving reporter. The roving reporter moved about during the game, recording activity and conversations, and asking questions that would illuminate the purposes and plans of the players.

SIMULAND

The players, twenty in all, were graduate students and undergraduate honors students in political science. Both groups were relatively knowledgeable concerning the problems of national development. For the undergraduates, the simulation exercise came as the climax to a semester course oriented toward the problems of development.

The first three hours of the exercise were hours of shifting alliances, free-wheeling negotiations, and attempts to form coalitions that could oust the government. On two occasions, the government, based on the support of the gentry, came close to falling, only to be saved by the skillful manner in which the President played the different elements of an opposition coalition against one another.

The Communists played a central role in the early stages of the game by their maneuvering against the government. With considerable enthusiasm, they began with a round of negotiations designed to probe for discontent on which they could base an anti-government coalition. The intelligentsia were attentive to Communist blandishments, and intrigued by the thought that the support of military branch B might be won away from the government into an alliance with the Communists and the intelligentsia. The alliance was never consummated, however, and difficulty arose over the question of who would control the new government once the old government was ousted. Throughout the negotiations with the Communists the intelligentsia had kept channels open to the government, and were finally persuaded not to oppose the government.

The President, during this period, had endeavored to hold his alliance firm without allowing it any real influence on governmental policy. He wanted to retain the support of military branch A and military branch B while discouraging the two from forming a firm enough alliance to dominate the government. The device used to drive a wedge between the two was the threat (or promise) of a treaty with the neighboring country of Lambda. Such a pact would run contrary to the interests of military A and was favored by military B on the grounds that reduction of the military threat would make possible increased governmental expenditures in the regions important to B. The President correctly assumed that military A was sufficiently committed to the government for it not to withdraw its support despite its disapproval of the treaty policy; and that military B would be sufficiently attracted by the possibility of a pact for it to avoid casting its lot with an anti-government coalition. In communicating with military A, the President stressed that the pact was "still tentative and unsigned," while, in communicating with military B, he referred to the pact as "still being negotiated strenuously."

By the process of divide and rule, the government staved off the challenge of the Communist-led coalition. Following the defeat, the Communists' influence on the game waned rapidly. Apparently, they had exhausted the sources of potential support open to them, and, from this point on, had nowhere to go.

In the next phase of the game, the intelligentsia and the commercial and entrepreneurial elite formed an alliance in opposition to the government but, lacking military support, had no way to force the government from office. An important break came with a request by military A for a conference with the intelligentsia and the entrepreneurial elite. Military A extracted important concessions for its support, including the agreement of the other partners that they would oppose the pact with Lambda and agree to the cessation of negotiations if the bid for power was successful. Military A agreed that the leaders of the intelligentsia should have important positions in a new government. To satisfy the intelligentsia, it was agreed that they should hold prominent positions in the new government and, to satisfy the commercial elite, it was agreed that the Communists should be completely excluded both from the alliance and from any new government. That is, rejection of Communist support became one of the grounds on which the three elite groups could agree.

The threat to the government from the emerging coalition seemed very real; however, the high point in the coalition's prospects soon passed. The formula on which the disparate elements had agreed was not enough to hold the alliance together. The entrepreneurial elite was troubled by the evident desire of the intelligentsia for extensive land reform, nationalization of foreign industries, and removal of government controls over unions. They were also troubled by what would become of a large loan they had made to the government should the government fall. The intelligentsia split into "idealist" and "realist" factions over whether the required compromises were worth it. The realists argued that the objective of overthrowing the government was worth the concessions, while the idealists argued that if the concessions were made the revolution would be betrayed at its birth, and the new government would be dominated by rightists rather than liberals. The dissent of the left wing intellectuals weakened the efforts of the intelligentsia to hold the alliance together and give it leadership. At this juncture the first half of the game ended.

As the second period began, a new pro-government coalition emerged, from which the intelligentsia were excluded by more or less mutual consent. The game, to this point, had a rightward drift. The early Communist-dominated alliance was replaced by a coalition dominated by the intelligentsia which, in turn, was succeeded by a distinctly right-wing alliance. The polarization process was now far advanced, and the remainder of the game was a story of attempts by the Communists and the intelligentsia to overthrow the government against the combined weight of the remaining elements in the game. The Communists undertook a campaign of terrorism and rioting (the extent of which was announced by the experimenters) which strengthened rather than weakened the hand of the government since it solidified the conservative elements behind the government. The more militant and radical the left became, the more tightly the conservative elements closed ranks. The intelligentsia sought to get support for their plans from the bureaucracy, but without notable success. Throughout the exercise, the bureaucracy functioned as an arm of the presidency, and never embarked on a really independent policy.

As the game approached its conclusion, the left wing forces, having failed to broaden their basis of political support, attempted a *coup d'état*. It was a long shot, and when the game procedures for a *coup* were followed, the attempt failed badly. The game ended with the government more firmly entrenched in power than it had been at the beginning, with the elite elements in Simuland ideologically polarized, and with the left wing in a weak and insecure position.

ANALYSIS OF SIMULAND

Reporting. As Sidney Verba has remarked, the investigator has almost total access to the history of the world that he simulates.* He can photograph or tape-record the entire experience, measure attitudes, read messages, ask leading questions of the performers while "history" is unfolding, and interview at length before and after the run. Such extensive analysis is, of course, a substantial undertaking. A danger in the analysis of a simulation run, as in the analysis of history itself, is that the *ex post facto* narrative of events may end in making events appear more symmetrical and behavior more rational and planned than in fact they were. The danger of a seriously slanted viewpoint can be overcome to some extent by increasing the number of autonomous accounts of the game. Consequently, in later exercises we used more than one reporter.

Role Playing. In a simulation involving players, there is room for great variation in the extent to which the roles of individual players are prescribed. Roles can be highly structured, leaving the player relatively little freedom of action, or they can be a loose fit, leaving the player a good deal of room for improvisation. Roles in the Simuland exercise fell toward the middle of the continuum. Elite roles were specified, but the particular interests of each actor were not. Because individual roles were not prescribed, dissension among members of the same elite was not built into the game. The disagreements which did emerge during the course of the game represented differences of opinion as to where the interest of the elite as a whole lay rather than differences based on calculations of individual interest.

Having a number of players cooperate in playing the part of a single elite has the advantage of simplicity, but it also introduces a somewhat unrealistic element. In Simuland, it meant that there would be less fragmentation and division among the elites than would normally be found in a developing society. It is interesting, however, that, despite the way the game was structured, fragmentation did emerge, particularly within the intelligentsia. As a result of the use of monolithic elites, players probably directed more attention to the broad problems faced by a developing country, and probably learned less about intra-elite frictions, bargaining, and compromise than they would have otherwise.

*"Simulation, Reality, and Theory in International Relations," *World Politics* (Vol. 16, No. 3, April, 1964), p. 501.

Associated with the use of monolithic elites was the absence of role conflict. The members of each elite were relatively impervious to arguments or appeals from other groups. In actual practice, many actors would have had overlapping membership in several groups and would have felt drawn in several directions simultaneously. The monolithic nature of the elites was tempered only by the existence of pre-existing personal friendships that cut across group lines to some extent.

Communications. The communications arrangements established by the experimenters are likely to have a profound impact on the movement of any game. The fact that the President and the members of the bureaucracy had free movement, and members of the elites did not, was of great advantage to the government. This gave the government a superior communications network, and allowed it to operate on the basis of more complete information than was possessed by the elites.

This exercise also suggests that the effect of face-to-face communication may be quite different from that of written communication in political situations. Chicanery and deception were much more common among players whose communication was exclusively through the written medium than among players who communicated by word of mouth. The players seemed aware of this, and preferred oral communication to written, not only because it moved more rapidly, but also because they appeared to feel greater confidence in the reliability of agreements reached in face-to-face discussion.

This kind of communication increases trust among players, but the introduction of too much of it would represent a distortion of reality. In retrospect, for example, it appears that the experimenters allowed too much face-to-face contact toward the end of the exercise. Physical movement from room to room became so free that it ceased to simulate closely the actuality of communications in a developing country. Political groups rarely enjoy full and free communication with one another, and the leaders of one group rarely have a full understanding of the purposes of leaders of other groups. If reality is to be approximated, therefore, the design and administration of a game must simulate these differentials in communication.

Congruence of the Game with Reality. One of the political features of a developing country that the exercise simulated quite well was the differential perceptions on the part of various actors. It was not easy for the players to keep up with what was going on in the game, with the consequence that there were widely divergent views of what was happening, of the significance of various events, and of the purposes of other actors. With a longer playing time, perceptions might have shown a tendency to stabilize or, perhaps, to polarize.

The exercise also highlighted the way in which knowledge and expertise can be translated into influence in a political situation. Those players who had studied the game carefully beforehand, who had read extensively about developing countries, and had planned their strategy ahead of time emerged quickly as dominant figures in the game.

Because the political predispositions of the players would necessarily affect the game, we attempted to assign roles to players on the basis of their political preferences. This was done on the assumption that an individual who could sympathize or identify with a particular role would find it easier to play that role effectively. In this and other exercises, it became clear that an individual normally finds it harder to bring energy, conviction, and imagination to a role that is uncongenial than to one that he can identify with.

The course of the game was heavily affected by the personalities and skills of the players. Players who were determined, interested, and politically inclined tended to direct other players. This is also true of full-scale politics, to be sure, but since simulation exercises involve relatively few players, exceptional weakness or strength among a few players can affect the entire movement of the game.

A distortion inherent in the game as it was played should be mentioned. It lay in the fact that the population of Simuland lived only a political life and had no personal interests. In real political situations, apathy, family ties, social status, and other nonpolitical factors have a great impact upon the course of political events. While private motivations could be introduced into more complex games than Simuland, a game will always emphasize those aspects of human affairs that the experimenters are interested in at the expense of other aspects.

A feature of Simuland that, under some circumstances, would be unrealistic was the degree to which the game was government oriented. The issues that absorbed the attention of the players were those relating to the success of the government in maintaining a viable coalition, the government's success in financing its growth and program, and whether or not a *coup* would be successful. The government was the most important feature of Simuland, and dominated the political life of the country. In some developing countries the government plays a role as prominent as that, but in many others it does not.

Another feature of Simuland was that the political system operated without political parties. Elites were the active elements, and conflict in the game was conflict among elites. Again, this pattern would be appropriate for some developing countries, but not for others. Political parties may take shape relatively late in the process of development, and they may, of course, emerge by easy stages from within elites or from among a coalition of elites. There were indications that, had the exercise continued longer, the experimenters might have witnessed the emergence of stable coalitions having some of the central characteristics of political parties. The authors were intrigued by the idea that it might be possible to simulate and observe the emergence of political parties from nonparty situations.

Finally, in Simuland, as in other simulation exercises, there was a tendency toward instability. However involved he is in the role he is to play, a player is always aware that it is a "game," and that no serious consequences to himself and his family will follow if he gambles in the game and loses. He may be inclined to behave irresponsibly because he is deeply involved in the game and wants to "win," or because he is bored and wants to break out of his role in search of entertainment. In this game, the tendency toward instability was offset fairly well by the manipulative skill of the President and a provision of the rules penalizing any unsuccessful attempt at a *coup d'état*. The designers of a game of this kind need to be aware of the problem of inherent instability, but if the game is well constructed and challenging, the problem can be overcome.

CONCLUSION

The Simuland exercise had its shortcomings, but it demonstrated beyond any doubt that player simulation of the processes of a developing country is feasible. It demonstrated also that players had little difficulty coping with an exercise of a moderate degree of complexity. The excitement the exercise generated among the players, and the attention the players applied to studying the scenario and playing the game, suggest that simulation of national systems has real merit as a training and instructional device.

2

POLITICAL DEVELOPMENT IN SIMULAND

RULES OF THE GAME

PURPOSE

The game is intended to simulate the interplay among the active political elites of a hypothetical society in the process of economic development.

SIMULAND

The hypothetical society is to be called Simuland, and the exercise will be supervised by a set of experimenters. The experimenters will also play the roles of certain actors who are not central to the game.

ORIENTATION PAPER

An orientation paper provides historical background and current information on Simuland's domestic political situation and foreign relations. The purposes of the paper are to suggest the character and interests of the elites, and to raise concrete problems and issues.

THE ACTORS

The active political elements in Simuland are:

The government
The bureaucracy and the police; job holders

The landed gentry and religious groups
The commercial and industrial leadership
The intelligentsia and students
Military branch A
Military branch B
The Communist Party

Each of the active political elements, with the exception of the government, will be called an elite. Each member is assumed to wield a proportionate share of the elite's power. Decisions for an elite must be taken on the basis of majority rule. In a situation threatening the government with peaceful or violent overthrow, a member of the elite may withhold his consent. (These provisions are introduced so as to avoid giving the impression that the elites are monolithic.)

THE MASSES

The masses are assumed to be essentially passive. They will respond only to stimuli: in the absence of activation by an elite group, will not act on their own. Mass support, therefore, will be one of the factors affecting the strength of an elite.

The masses will be played by the experimenters. That is, the experimenters will examine the nature of an elite appeal to the masses, and assess the degree of success it is likely to enjoy.

THE FOREIGN ENVIRONMENT

There are three countries in the foreign environment of Simuland: the United States, the Soviet Union, and Lambda, Simuland's neighbor. The roles of these countries will be played by the experimenters.

The government of Simuland may solicit economic and military aid from the United States or the Soviet Union and these countries may deny the request, grant it unconditionally, or attach political and economic conditions to granting it. The government of Simuland is, of course, free to accept or reject such conditions.

Potential effects of the foreign environment may be threefold: (i) Military aid may increase the power of the military; (ii) economic aid may be used to improve the economic position of an elite or the masses; and (iii) issues concerning foreign countries may be exploited by any elite.

Only the government may negotiate with foreign countries, but the elites are free to try to influence governmental decisions.

THE GOVERNMENT

It is the responsibility of the government to establish policies and programs for Simuland. These must be decided upon with an eye to the degree of elite and mass support each policy is likely to generate. Policy making will normally proceed, therefore, in the context of the political and economic support the government desires from the elites.

The most important policy-making focus of the government is on the preparation of the annual budget.

The President will be drawn from one of the elites. At the beginning of the game he will be from the gentry, an arrangement which may change as the game proceeds. He conducts the affairs of the government in conjunction with the bureaucracy, and is housed, with the bureaucracy, in the government office.

THE BUDGET

The President, as head of the government, must obtain sufficient support for his budget, or he may be overthrown.

The income sources in the budget are: (i) Personal, land, and corporate taxes upon the gentry; (ii) personal, land, and corporate taxes upon the entrepreneurs; (iii) foreign grants; (iv) loans from gentry and entrepreneurs; and (v) consumption taxes.

The President's choices for *expenditure* are: (i) Military; (ii) administration; (iii) welfare; (iv) investment in agriculture and industry; and (v) special expenditures or subsidies.

In a given year, expenditures cannot exceed total income.

STRATEGY PAPER

Periodically, each elite and the government will submit a strategy paper to the experimenters. Policy not appropriate to the situation as presented in the orientation paper, or illogical, given the position of the elite, will not be deemed by the experimenters to add to the strength of an elite. If a player is uncertain whether a given program or policy falls within the confines of the game, he should seek the views of the experimenters.

The strategy paper must be signed by at least two members of the elite. The experimenters will note whether a paper is signed by two members or three members as a means of assessing the degree of unity within that elite. The paper will be organized under five headings:

Actions taken, appeals made, and programs initiated
A record of such actions as the formation of a coalition, taken in

consultation with other elites. The conditions of any agreement must be set forth.

Appeals to and programs for the masses

Specify the segment of the masses to which the appeal is addressed (i.e. peasantry or urban masses), and the content of the appeal, program, or policy.

Appeals to other elites

Specify the elite, and the policy, program, or psychological appeal involved.

Allocation of financial resources (to be filled out by the gentry and commercial and industrial elite only.) Funds will be allotted to each of the financial elites at the beginning of the game. These represent the annual return on the very large sums each elite has invested at home in the past. [The same base sum will be made available at the beginning of each year, and to it will be added an increment proportionate to the country's rate of growth.] This income has not yet been taxed, however, so that an elite will not know the amount of its investible capital until after the government has established its tax policy.

The elites have four alternative uses for this capital:

    (a) capital export—anticipated yield, 7 per cent
    (b) domestic investment—anticipated yield, 4 per cent
    (c) savings (hoarding)—no financial return
    (d) loans to the government—terms negotiable.

Investible capital may be divided among these uses in any way. The financial gain of the elite during the year will be calculated on the basis of the amounts invested at the different rates of return.

The investible sum at the beginning of the second year will consist of the base sum, plus the growth increment, plus the earnings of the first year minus taxes.

The investible sum at the beginning of the third year will consist of the base sum, plus the earnings of the second year minus taxes.

Confidential statements to the experimenters can also be made. Any difference between the real intentions of an elite and the intentions conveyed to the other players must be made clear to the experimenters. For example, if there was a secret understanding between two elites relating to an alliance, it should be stated here. Information concerning the covert strategies of an elite will not be communicated by the experimenters to the other elites.

ECONOMIC GROWTH

The rate of economic growth is related to the total annual investment, that is, to government investment, plus private investment, plus foreign investment. The larger the volume of total investment, the higher is the rate of economic development, ranging from 0 to 5 per cent.

THE PRESS

Each elite will submit multiple copies of its strategy paper. The non-secret elements of each strategy paper will be combined and circulated, along with official information from the experimenters and the press. It is through the press that the actions, plans, programs, and appeals of a given elite become known to the country as a whole.

At any point during the game, an elite may supply the experimenters with information (multiple copies) it wishes to have disseminated through the press. (For the convenience of the experimenters, the number of releases must not exceed three per period.)

COMMUNICATION

Inter-elite consultation is provided also by written communications and oral negotiations.

(i) *Written communication:* Communications among elites will normally be written, with a copy of each message going to the experimenters. Messages among elites are to be sent through the messenger service.

(ii) *Oral negotiation:* The President, or a member of the bureaucracy designated by him, may negotiate with whomever he pleases. Except for military A and military B, whom he can see jointly, all other negotiations must be bilateral. Negotiations should be kept as brief as possible.

An elite wishing to negotiate with another must submit a written request to the experimenters, stating the purpose of the negotiation. The experimenters will normally grant the request (subject to the limitations of space and traffic), and assign a place of meeting. The experimenters retain the right to monitor the discussion for their own purposes.

Only one member of an elite may be absent from elite headquarters at a given time for purposes of negotiation. However, this does not apply to the government.

ELITE ROLES

Throughout the game, each elite should keep in mind its character and interests as defined in the orientation paper. Adherence to designated interests does not rule out changes of policy, program, and outlook, but such changes should be congruent with the basic situation of each elite, and the basis for substantial changes should be made clear to the experimenters.

(i) *The bureaucracy* may make suggestions to the President and voice its policy preferences, but all governmental decision-making power rests with the President. Should the bureaucracy be militantly opposed to the President's policies, it may engage in minor harassment, but not in outright disobedience or falsification of records.

If, in carrying on government business, members of the bureaucracy have the opportunity to negotiate with members of other elites on matters of bureaucratic interest, they are free to do so. Independent actions taken by the bureaucracy must be agreed upon by both members.

(ii) *The landed gentry and religious groups* will, at the onset of the game, provide the President, who will reside in the government office. The remaining two members must consult their third colleague, the President, on all significant policy matters. In the event the government is overthrown, the ex-President will return to this group.

In addition to its normal political activities, the gentry must also allocate its financial resources, and note these allocations on the strategy sheet.

(iii) *The commercial and industrial leadership* must, in addition to its political activities, allocate its financial resources and indicate this allocation on the strategy sheet.

(iv) *The intelligentsia and students* can negotiate with other elites. They have, in addition, a capacity to communicate with the peasant and urban masses if they choose to make the effort.

(v, vi) *Military branch A and military branch B* are not wholly unified, as is common in developing countries. Each branch will be played by a separate team and will be treated as a distinct element.

The military branches have the special function of formulating policies relating to national security and of presenting them to the government.

(vii) *The Communist Party* may have difficulty in dealing with the other elites, but it has an unusual capacity for appealing to the peasants, the urban masses, and organized labor.

CHANGE OF GOVERNMENT

There are two types of governmental change.

(a) *Non-violent change that follows bargaining or an ultimatum:* This method does not involve the use of force, which means that the government must consent to its peaceful deposition. Change of this kind would normally result from an alteration in the elite alliance underlying the government, or a reduction in the mass support of the government.

Before a coalition may attempt to change the government, the elements in that coalition must signify (on change-of-government forms submitted to the experimenters) who is to become President if the government is ousted. This change can occur only at the end of a period, and is an orderly, negotiated change. In the event the President will not step down, even when faced with an elite coalition that is stronger than his regime, there is no recourse but violence.

(b) *Coup d'état:* This method requires that change-of-government papers be filed by one of the elites (or, in concert, by several elites). A bell is rung, and all other communication must cease until the governmental crisis is resolved.

Knowing only the identity of the elite which is attempting the *coup*, and such additional information as it may have gained in its negotiation, each elite must, within three minutes, file a change-of-government paper indicating whether it will support the government, support the attempted *coup*, or remain neutral.

The success of a *coup* will hinge on the strength of the government coalition in relation to the strength of the coalition trying to overthrow it. The experimenters will announce, as soon as possible, whether the attempted *coup* was successful. They will base their calculation on the ratio of "force points" between the contesting coalitions. The greater the differential, the more likely it is that the stronger group will prevail, but probability, not certainty, is involved, and therefore the outcome can never be fully assured. Thus, when forces are equal, the probability of rebel success is 0.5, while a rebel force twice the size of the government has a success probability of 0.8.

Once the probability has been determined, a die will be cast. An 0.5 probability means that a 4, 5, or 6 on the die will result in the success of the *coup*, while a 0.8 value means that a 2 through 6 on the die will result in rebel success.

A Situation Report will be given out at the end of each period to note the changes in the number of force points held by each elite.

Initial allocations include a hard-core level below which an elite's strength cannot fall, and are as follows:

Elite	Total Points	Hard Core Points
Military A	200	100
Military B	150	50
Landed gentry	150	100
Commercial elite	100	50
Intelligentsia	200	100
Communist Party	100	20
Bureaucracy	60	60

At the beginning of the game, and at the end of each period, force points will be allocated to each of the elites and to the government. Force points given at the beginning of a period will remain throughout the period. The force points possessed by an elite will vary with the changing support of the masses, the success or failure of policies and programs, and other variables. If, for example, the government budget was heavily weighted in the direction of increased government expenditures for the military, the military would receive additional force points at the beginning of the next period. By the same token, if the government received foreign military aid, this aid would strengthen the military and the government (provided the military backed the government).

A situation might develop in which the government would choose to concentrate its resources on a buildup of military forces, even though this concentration might create resentment among the masses. The government could calculate that the addition of 1000 soldiers to the armed forces would in terms of internal security, exactly offset the discontent these policies generated among 5000 of the masses. The addition of the 1000 soldiers would add 10 force points, while popular dissatisfaction would take away 10 force points.

Force points are allotted to the economic elites on the basis of both their political support and their changing financial position.

An unsuccessful attempt at a *coup* will not only discredit the offending elite, it will also result in a substantial reduction of its strength.

ORIENTATION PAPER: SIMULAND, YESTERDAY AND TODAY

I. HISTORY

In 1715, Simuland was conquered by a more advanced European nation, Alpha. Prior to that, Simuland had developed a relatively complex civilization, and was a formidable military power on her continent, having conquered territory constituting nearly twice her present size. Strife between Alpha and Gamma, another colonial power, was responsible for the sharp reduction in the size of Simuland. The old kingdom was divided between Alpha and Gamma by the Treaty of 1750.

During the colonial era, Simuland was directed by a state council in Alpha. Edicts of the council were executed in Simuland by a bureaucracy whose top ranks were Alphan, and whose lower ranks included members of the native aristocracy of Simuland. In order to assure efficient native administration, Alpha encouraged an education program in Simuland, but its benefits were restricted primarily to the aristocracy. At the time of independence, only 30 per cent of the native population was literate, and of this group only 10 per cent had an education beyond high school.

Before the arrival of the Alphans, the native religion was tied closely to the native gentry, who served as both the political and religious leaders of the people. The Alphans made nominal conversion to their religion mandatory, but only members of the gentry were inducted into the religious orders. The new religion simply continued to justify aristocratic rule, and it further elevated the native leaders above the masses. Today, as under Alphan colonial rule, church affairs are regulated by the government, which means that the gentry and the bureaucracy continue to dominate this department of the national life.

The overthrow of Alphan domination was accomplished with relatively little bloodshed. The radical leadership of the revolutionary movement was supplied by the Simuland intelligentsia, a handful of whom had been educated in Alpha. Impressive student-led demonstrations by urban workers in Capitol City were followed by the outbreak of sporadic terrorist actions, also led by students, in the western provinces. The bureaucracy played a quiet but important role in negotiations with Alphan officials throughout this period. Alpha was persuaded to yield, before the mounting tide of nationalism hit its peak, and in 1950 the formal transfer of sovereignty was made. The present head of government, a member of the gentry and leader of the negotiating bureaucrats, came to power at that time.

II. THE ECONOMIC AND SOCIAL SITUATION

Under Alphan rule, Simuland served as a source of agricultural products and raw materials for industrial use. Private companies, granted land by the Crown, established large estates for the cultivation of sugar and, to a lesser extent, cotton and coffee. In addition, a few Alphan entrepreneurs established processing factories in Simuland.

The agricultural sector of the economy still accounts for the majority of Simuland's Gross National Product, and is her major source of foreign exchange. Sugar alone comprises ⅔ of the value of her exports. In recent years, however, a glut on the world sugar market has led to efforts to make the country less dependent on one crop. While Simuland's agriculturalists have tried to convert sugar lands into more profitable hemp, the Soviet Union has helped tide the country over by taking its excess sugar in trade for industrial goods and technical assistance.

The traditional emphasis on production for export, at the expense of production for domestic needs, has created a severe dislocation. The need for a large volume of food imports has been a serious drain on the supply of foreign exchange. Recently, the United States has provided Simuland with wheat shipments under Public Law 480. Nevertheless, the high prices created by the food shortage have been strongly felt by the population, particularly the workers in Capitol City and other eastern cities.

Despite the continued predominance of agriculture, industrial development has proceeded quite rapidly, partly because of the stimulus provided by foreign industry. This foreign industry, owned largely by Alphan and United States interests, pays wages that are unusually high by Simuland standards. Suggestions that foreign industry be expropriated have, to date, been effectively countered with the argument that foreign industry is the most efficient sector of the economy and, furthermore, that its presence helps assure a continuing flow of military and economic assistance from the United States.

Only 13 per cent of Simuland's labor force is directly engaged in industry, but industry provides 20 per cent of the Gross National

Product. This industry is established predominantly in Capitol Province, in which Capitol City is located, and the two adjoining eastern provinces.

The lure of the city and industrial wages has led to a sharp increase in the population of Capitol City. The population of the city is now 2,500,000, a fourfold increase since 1900. The population boom has generated the typical problems of urban growth. Sewage facilities, public health facilities, and many other services are seriously inadequate. These problems are shared, to a somewhat lesser degree, by the other cities in the eastern part of the country.

Economists have pointed out two problems that impede rapid industrial development:

1. Electrical power is the obvious power source for Simuland's industry, but this resource is now inadequate for industrial expansion. Private industry has shown no inclination to develop electrical power, and the government has done nothing in this field.

2. The transportation system in Simuland is inadequate for present needs, let alone for future needs. The road and rail network in the vicinity of Capitol Province is fairly well developed, but in all other parts of the country it falls far short of present and future needs. This transportation gap has also inhibited the export of agricultural products.

III. THE POLITICAL SITUATION

The President has been in office since the achievement of independence in 1950. The basis of his power has been a coalition, albeit sometimes precarious, between the gentry and the commercial and industrial elite. On the whole, he has received the loyalty and support of the bureaucracy.

The President likes to point out that Simuland has enjoyed an annual growth rate of about 4 per cent over the past ten years. He customarily attributes this to his oft-stated interest in economic growth and the "vigorous" policies of his administration. His critics concede that the country has grown during his regime, but argue that more aggressive and imaginative leadership would make possible a substantially higher rate of growth. They argue further that the political basis of the President's regime prevents him from pursuing the kind of policies that would speed up economic growth, and that the country, therefore, cannot afford to retain him in power.

The structure of agriculture has changed very little since the departure of the Alphans. It is still based upon large estates and a highly paternalistic relationship between the owner and the individual peasant. There is little movement from one estate to another, and many peasants still tend to identify more with their landowner than with other peasants. This explains, simultaneously, one of the sources of the gentry's strength and the reason why other groups have had so little success, thus far, in organizing and activating the peasants politically. There are indications, however, that, when presented effectively, the issue of land reform has appeal and may serve as a focal point for diverse discontents.

In the cities, the growth of the trade union movement has more or less paralleled the growth of industry. At present the unions are closely controlled by the government. Any group wishing to form a union must receive a governmental charter, and all candidates for union office must be approved by the government. Of the 6,000,000 workers in Capitol Province, 1,500,000 are in the government-sponsored unions. Because of the gap between the government-approved union leaders and the rank and file, Communist agitation has found the union movement a fertile field for organization. Some estimates indicate that Communists and Communist sympathizers may comprise 50 per cent of the union membership.

Despite this organizational success, however, the Communist leadership in Simuland has been sharply divided during the last two years on a series of policy questions. The Sino-Soviet split has had serious repercussions within the movement, and the cleavage on this question fairly closely parallels an old split between the more militant and less militant Simuland Communists. The radical members of the leadership are prepared to go ahead with strikes, riots, and subversion even at the price of the party's being outlawed. Others argue that the advantages the Communist Party derives from being able to operate as a legal organization vastly outweigh any gains that might accrue from illegal activity.

An interesting new phenomenon is the growth in the number of independent workers' societies. By taking on some of the protective coloring of social groups, these societies have avoided the need for a government charter. Their orientation tends to be of a non-Communist, socialist variety. Leadership is provided by students and members of the intelligentsia.

From the standpoint of national security, the gap in military readiness between Simuland and her neighbor, Lambda, is alarming to some. A rivalry between the two countries persists, since it was

Lambda which inherited much of the Simuland territory lost through the Treaty of 1750. At present Lambda is governed by a military dictatorship.

A split of some years standing in Simuland's military forces further weakens the position of the country. Branch A is located in the eastern part of the country, which includes Capitol Province. Many of its officers are from the commercial and industrial families in the area. Branch B is located in the western part of the country; its officers are largely from the gentry and its conscripts from the peasantry. Branch A, increasingly disturbed about the national security situation, since Lambda borders on Simuland in the east, has urged the government to negotiate for foreign military aid. Branch B agrees with the government that branch A is exaggerating the foreign threat. The officers' corps of branch B shares the mistrust that the President has for branch A. It feels that a strong branch A might represent a threat to the government, which, of course, means a threat to the special position of the gentry. It agrees with the widespread feeling in the west that the eastern part of the country is already prosperous and populous, and now hopes to dominate the country once branch A achieves military supremacy.

STRATEGY PAPER

I. *Political Strategy* To be filled out by all elites and the government. Only nonconfidential information should be included. (8 copies) Actions taken in collaboration with other elements (coalitions, their terms, etc.), and appeals to the masses and to other elites.

Appeals being made, programs being initiated, etc.

II. *Allocation of financial resources* (to be filled out by the gentry and the commercial and industrial elite).

Total disposable income _____

(a) Capital export (anticipated return, 5 per cent) _____

(b) Domestic investment (anticipated return, 4 per cent) _____

(c) Savings and miscellaneous allocations of funds (Please explain any special allocations) _____

(d) Loans to government (rate subject to negotiation) _____

Total _____

(Should equal total disposable income)

Comments: _____

_____

_____

Signatures of Agreement   1. _____

2. _____

3. _____

CHANGE-OF-GOVERNMENT FORM

I. *Nonviolent change*
    - (a) Elite from which the new President will come _____
    - (b) Points cast: For the government _____
        - For the opposition _____

II. *Coup d'état*
    - (a) Elite leading the *coup* _____
    - (b) Points allocated: In support of the coup _____
        - In support of the government _____
        - (Uncommitted points do not enter
        - into calculations)

For elite _____   Force points available _____

Signatures of Agreement   1. _____

2. _____

3. _____

3

THE BRAZILIAN SIMULATION

The Simuland exercise demonstrated the possibility of inventing a country and simulating certain of the developmental processes of that hypothetical country. For training purposes and, perhaps, for studying prototypical situations, the use of hypothetical countries is valuable. There is an upper limit to the complexity possible in such a simulate, however, because of the difficulty of fabricating data of the kind and quantity needed. There is a real danger, furthermore, that inconsistencies will creep in, and that characteristics that are mutually incompatible will be given to the country. Also, there is no standard by which one can compare the realism of player actions or the outcome of an exercise.

After reflecting on these problems, we decided to simulate an actual developing nation rather than a hypothetical one. For this, one would not need to invent a history for the country, a political system, a set of actors and institutions, and assorted data. One would simply study an actual society, and deal with its characteristics, its personages, and their interrelationships. If additional facts were needed, real data rather than imaginative estimates could be used.

Robert Daland of the University of North Carolina Department of Political Science became interested in the simulation experiments at this juncture. Since he had recently returned from a 2-year visit to Brazil, and since fairly good data on Brazil were available, the decision was made to simulate the politico-economic processes of that country. Professor Daland's contribution to the game was of critical importance. Campus directors of a Peace Corps training program for Latin America, willing to experiment with simulation as a training

26

tool, gave encouragement and financial support to the venture. Because the tight schedule of the trainees allowed little time for familiarization with Brazil and the rules of the game, the designers were limited in the degree of complexity they could incorporate into the exercise.

A major difficulty in the preparation of the Brazilian scenario was the dearth of sophisticated, published, political analyses of the Brazilian political system. Political science is scarcely established as a discipline in Brazil, and such research as has been done has largely centered on structural and legal questions. Despite the relative absence of analytic materials, we tried to achieve an overall understanding of the Brazilian political system, and to relate that system to the growing body of political and social theory.

Construction of a working model of Brazil began with the recognition that conflicting pressures and overlapping group memberships were central to the Brazilian situation. The authors realized that this complexity could not be accommodated if the monolithic elites of Simuland were to be adhered to. Instead of starting off with a series of elites, as in Simuland, the designers took the individual leader as the basic unit in the game. A leader was perceived, however, as playing a number of different roles. He might be a member of a political party, of the legislature, or of an interest group; he might be associated with the military, or he might be a leader in the church. Therefore, a group, such as a political party, was composed of the actors who had a party role. But while each party member had a party role, he also had other roles that might either reinforce his party activity or conflict with it. In the game, then, a party was not a monolithic organization of dedicated members, but an assemblage of individuals who, because of party and other allegiances, might well give priority to some interest other than that of party.

With this approach, each actor had to be given an identity. Because of the special importance of certain leaders in Brazil, surrogates of these actors were introduced into the game. Players adopted the roles of President Branco, Governors Pinto, Lacerda, and de Barros, General Kruel, and a few others. The remaining players were composite identities: prototypes—industrialists, mine owners, land owners, military officers, middle-class leaders, labor leaders, peasant league organizers, churchmen. In addition, an effort was made to simulate a population that would approximate the actual population of Brazil and represent the major political and economic interests.

All actors, whether playing real or representative roles, were assigned a set of attitudes on major issues, were given primary and secondary economic interests, and were sometimes given special loyalties and attachments. Within this general framework of attitudes, interests, and attachments, however, players were free to act their parts as they saw fit. Each player had to establish a set of priorities concerning the goals he would pursue, the time and energy he would devote to each goal, and the strategy he would follow in seeking that goal.

An active group life was encouraged by the design of the game. Certain groups (such as the political parties) were built into the game to begin with. As the focus of the game shifted, however, and as new issues and problems became salient, new groups and coalitions were expected to emerge. Because of the relatively large number of players, and the diversity of objectives, interests, and strategies of these players, the range of potential groups in the game was almost infinite.

A question central to the construction of the game concerned the basis on which players were to be grouped together. An analysis of the political situation in Brazil led us to conclude that the basic organizing principle in this simulate should not be elite membership, as in Simuland, but the geographical region. In a single region, therefore, were grouped military men, property owners, political leaders, and others. Since Brazil has a large number of states, it was necessary to simplify the geographical organization of the simulate somewhat, retaining the larger states, but aggregating the smaller. Thus, for example, Rio Grande do Sul, São Paulo, and Minas Gerais were represented, but others were aggregated into the "States of the Interior" (See map, p. 68). Players were assigned to each region in accordance with the political, economic, and military distribution of each type in that region. For example, Senor Theta lived in Minas Gerais and represented the mining interests of that state. In the Northeast, lived Senor Pi, a cacao producer, and Senor Sigma, a leader of the Peasant League.

Communication among players within a region was, therefore, easy. Communication was also allowed along party and professional lines. Political leaders met face to face in party caucuses, and military leaders were able to meet at the *Clube Militar*. All players could communicate by written messages. The mass media were represented by a newspaper and by Radio Brazil (a public address system).

The experience with Simuland showed that the communications system in a simulate is of great importance to the outcome of the simulation exercise. The point was to be driven home again in the case of Brazil. The ease of communication, and, hence, of coordination, among the military leaders through the *Clube Militar* helps explain why the role of the military was so important in the simulation exercise. Freedom of movement was also an important resource for the governors. They lacked military power, economic power, and budgetary power, but, because they could move about, they were able to translate their capacity to communicate with each other into political influence.

Having decided upon the actors in the system, the basic principle of organization, and the main channels of communication, our next task was to devise ways of incorporating the electoral system, the legislature, and the executive branch. An analysis of Brazilian voting showed that, to a very considerable extent, individual voters take their cues from leaders. Elections in Brazil are won or lost, depending on the coalitions formed among leaders. In addition, a provision restricting the vote to the literate substantially reduces the size of the electorate. This meant, we calculated, that, if the leaders were polled, and if a weighting were applied to the vote of each, it would be roughly equivalent to the size of the following each enjoyed; an election could then be satisfactorily simulated in the game.

The legislature was incorporated into the game in a simplified form. The bicameral legislature of Brazil was transformed into a single-house legislature. Certain actors were designated as members of the legislature, and these individuals met periodically in legislative session. Since the players so designated were also members of political parties, they represented the different party factions in the legislature. The party composition of the simulated legislature reflected the composition of the Brazilian legislature, except that minor parties were omitted or collapsed together. A system of weighted voting was instituted to make certain that no party had a disproportionate voting weight in the miniature legislature.

The executive branch was incorporated in the form of a President and several ministers. The President of Brazil is a powerful policy-making force, and the arrangements built into the game were designed to concede him this position of prominence without, at the same time, allowing him to dominate the exercise.

Since we were primarily interested in this exercise as a political simulate, we were content to oversimplify the functioning of the Brazilian economy radically. Only the public aspects of the economy were incorporated. No arrangements were made to give the players private economic lives. The government plan and the budget were combined into a single budgetary unit. To achieve congruence to the actual processes in Brazil, the budget process in the game was made as complex as seemed feasible, given the limited opportunity that the players would have to become familiar with the game before playing. In another exercise, much more could be done to incorporate the richness and complexity of the Brazilian economy. As it was, debate was to center, first, around a tentative government plan, then around an agreed one, and, finally, on the actual government expenditures (which might or might not be according to the agreed plan).

The revenues received by the government, reflecting previous governmental policies, would be calculated by the experimenters and communicated to the President. Deficit spending was possible; indeed, the experimenters assumed that the government, to satisfy the diverse demands made upon it, would have to resort to that kind of spending. A mechanism for simulating inflation was built into the game, with the rate of inflation dependent, in part, upon the amount of deficit spending. The impact of inflation was differential, bearing more heavily on some players than others. Foreign aid was available if the government of Brazil could persuade the foreign actors to make grants or loans. The external environment included the United States, various international banking agencies; Cuba, and several other Communist countries. While some of the foreign actors tried to influence political developments within "Brazil," their contributions were generally confined to the economic sphere.

The goal was to simulate, not the economy of Brazil, but the controversy centering around the political and economic issues, and the political consequences of the functioning of the Brazilian economy. In constructing this part of the simulate, assumptions had to be made concerning such matters as the role of investment and the impact of inflation. The basis for these assumptions was not always as sound as we would have liked; therefore, in a later exercise some of them might be changed.

One of the problems facing those who attempt societal simulation is how to build into the simulate the physical action that is supposed to take place. How, within the confines of a game, can a demonstration, a riot, or a *coup* take place? Another problem is how a sequence of physical actions—the initial action, a response to it, a response to that, etc.—can take place in a game without being preprogrammed or decreed by the experimenters.

The purpose of the exercise was not to simulate physical action but deliberation, negotiation, interpersonal and intergroup relations, and decision making. Therefore, it is not physical action that needs to be simulated, but the political consequences of it. This eases the task greatly, and opens up the possibility that a simulation exercise might be rather like a stage play in which the battles take place off-stage and are recounted to the players by breathless messengers arriving periodically from the front.

On the second point, we felt the players could allow for action and response if they reduced all action to a sequence of steps. Thus, in order to take action in the Brazilian game, an actor had to inform the experimenters of the first step in the proposed action, the second step, and so on, together with the time intervals between steps. The experimenters would approve the action if it were within the capabilities of the actors involved. When approved, the initial action would be assumed to have taken place at the time indicated. The experimenters would announce the action, and inquire what counteraction, if any, the other actors wished to take. Information on the counteraction would then be communicated to the first actor so that he might modify the second action in the sequence he had planned. The following might be such a sequence of events:

4:00 General A orders an alert of the troops under his command.
4:10 The President denounces the action and alerts other military units in Brazil.
4:15 The troops of General A move northward along the Coast. General A delivers an ultimatum to the President.
4:20 Troops under command of the President, significantly outnumbering those of General A, confront the latter at the border of Guanabara. The President demands the surrender of General A and his troops.
4:25 General A refuses to surrender, saying he owes it to the people of Brazil to bring the administration to a recognition of its errors.
4:35 The President announces that his representatives have met with General A, that orders have been given to troops on both sides to avoid hostilities, and that efforts are being made to achieve a political settlement of difficulties.

In this sequence, a crisis arises, and both sides take physical actions while simultaneously negotiating actively for political support. Ultimately, in keeping with Brazilian practice, a political settlement is achieved, with little or no blood being spilled. Most physical action having broad political consequences for a nation takes place over a period of days or weeks. The step-by-step procedure slows down the action so that it may be incorporated in a simulation exercise, and so that there may be time for response as events begin to unfold.

One of our objectives was to have the game structured in a way that would parallel the political situation in Brazil. Ideally, players should feel roughly the same set of constraints in the game that they would feel in Brazil. Since the political situation in Brazil is very fluid, a tightly knit game would have distorted reality. The Brazilian Constitution and the political rules of the game allow a wide range of behavioral options; therefore, so should the game. Since what is legal and illegal is often uncertain in Brazil, a good deal of room is left for boldness and initiative. During the game, for example, when the election results were unsatisfactory to the President, he calmly ruled that there had been fraud in one state, and voided the votes cast there. If one asks what strategies in the game are available to this individual or to that elite, the answer—if the game has been properly constructed—may be that there is the same range of strategies in the game as there would be for that particular individual or elite in Brazil. That is to state an ideal, of course, but, as the complexity of the game is increased, the ideal may come close to being realized.

THE GAME

The Brazilian exercise was played in the fall of 1964. Approximately 65 persons, including a core group of 32 Peace Corps trainees, were involved in it. The game ran for 7 hours, and the major foci of attention were: The budget and the government plan; the campaign and the election; and the threat of a military *coup*.

In the first hour of the game, the government was preoccupied with its budget. The budget-making process was highly political, with allocations being determined on the basis of the political strength of the various interest groups and the degree of support they would pledge the government. The receipt of economic aid from the United States eased the strain on the budget and made the President's task of balancing the budget easier than it otherwise would have been. The success of the President and his cabinet in getting foreign aid (not anticipated by the experimenters), served to reduce the financial and political pressures on the government.

Even while the attention of the government was directed toward the budget, efforts were under way to form a right wing coalition, centering around the UDN and PSD parties. This coalition worked with some effect during the sessions of the legislature. The budget recommended by the President was approved by the legislature with relatively few changes. The leaders of the military were upset that their allocation was below the level they desired. This may have been the beginning of the military's alienation from the government, a feature that was to persist through the first half of the game.

News that the President was planning to create a new army further antagonized some of the military leaders, and it was at this time that the first discussion of a possible *coup* took place. The President, told of the discontent of the military, soon let it be known that he was dropping the plan for a new army, and planning a generous increase in the military's budgetary allocation for the following year. Individual military leaders had concluded by now, however, that the government was moving toward the left, and was unsympathetic to the needs of the military. Their concern was not eased by labor strikes, in three central and southern states, designed to force the government to play a more active role in the welfare field. Discussions envisioning a broadly based anti-government coalition continued to take place, even as the attention of most players turned once more to the preparation of the annual budget.

1965 BUDGET

Category		Level of Satisfaction	Government Proposal	Congress Resolution
I.	Regional Division: NE and Interior States	55	40	40
II.	Regional Division: Central and Southern States	145	115	145
III.	Sector Division: Agriculture	85	60	60
IV.	Sector Division: Industry	80	60	60
V.	Military Expenditures	175	150	140
VI.	Bureaucrats	75	70	55
VII.	Repayment Foreign Debt	73	73	73

To strengthen his position to meet the growing threat from the military, the President designed a budget to win the support of the middle and lower classes. Governor Pinto pledged the full support of Minas Gerais to the government.

Military leaders were thrown into confusion by the announcement over Radio Brazil that President Branco had accused General Alpha of insubordination, removed him from his post as Military Commander of Guanabara, and replaced him with General Beta. Generals Alpha, Iota, and Kruel viewed this move by the government as a step toward the left, and as an effort to weaken and discredit the military. They felt that the prestige and position of the military were being challenged in a frontal way, and that they had no alternative but to respond. Accordingly, they alerted their troops to march on the Capital, and dispatched a note to President Branco, demanding that he remove General Beta from office and turn him over to the military to be court-martialed for insubordination.

As the crisis deepened, discussions took place between President Branco and the rightist military leaders. Behind the scenes, the military were planning for the *coup*, and the President was busily trying to isolate the military by drawing off civilian support from the generals. Here, the experimenters made it clear that they would block any attempted *coup* by the generals, on the ground that in Brazil generals would not, in fact, proceed without significant civilian backing. President Branco, in a conference with Generals Alpha, Iota, and Kruel, offered to reinstate General Alpha and remove General Beta. For the first time, effective communication between the two factions was achieved. The crisis, thereafter, eased rapidly, and a basis for future collaboration began to take shape.

Throughout this crisis and the tense moments that were to follow, the normal processes of government went on. The government prepared its budgets, and the legislature debated them along with other matters. Among the measures the legislature acted on were a land reform bill, a tax on unused land, an increase in corporate taxes, and a decrease in income taxes.

As the 1969 elections approached, it became clear to President Branco that his UDN/PSD/PSP coalition did not have enough votes to defeat the PTB/PSB coalition. The President had decided before the election that he would level charges of "electoral irregularities" in São Paulo, and void the election returns from that state. Such a move would guarantee victory for his coalition, and he would rely on General Kruel to deal with any violence that it might cause.

Just prior to the election, President Branco, at the request of Generals Alpha and Kruel, announced that General Beta had been relieved of all military duties. Thus, the leftist coalition was deprived of all significant military resources.

The results of the election, announced at 3:52, were: PTB—51; PSD-UDN—48. The plan of invalidating the election results from São Paulo was now put into effect, General Kruel's troops moving in to occupy that state. The votes were voided, and the tabulation, minus those votes, was now: PSD-UDN—37; PTB—31. Pinto, the candidate agreed upon by the generals and President Branco, took office as the new President, and appointed a cabinet, suggested largely by Generals Psi, Iota, Alpha, and Kruel. All military units were alerted to suppress riots or strikes, and the military announced its total support of President Pinto, and its determination to maintain law and order. The rest of the game was spent bargaining for ministerial posts and deciding on future policies, most decisions being strongly influenced by General Kruel and the military.

ANALYSIS

The Brazilian simulate was designed primarily as a teaching exercise, and, in that respect, was an almost unqualified success. To help evaluate the game, a questionnaire was administered to the Peace Corps trainees at the conclusion. Twenty of the 23 respondents felt that the exercise had added to their knowledge of Brazil; the other 3 gave answers which, though qualified, were still affirmative. To the more important question, "Did the game help you gain an understanding of the process of development?", 20 respondents again gave an unqualified "yes"; only 1 answered "no". Nineteen of them indicated that "the time spent on the game was more useful than an equivalent amount of class time," while only 1 felt that it had been less useful.*

To be sure, after 10 weeks of intensive classroom training, almost any change would have seemed an improvement. Nevertheless, the players did succeed in becoming deeply involved in the game, and involvement is often an important precondition for effective learning. Players, no doubt, learned something about Brazil. More important-

*Other open-ended questions included: "Do you think that simulation exercises might be incorporated as a normal part of the Peace Corps training program?" Clearly affirmative, 17; qualified affirmative (Yes, but . . .), 4; negative, 0; did not answer, 2. "Do you think the game was useful as a training and educational exercise?" Clearly affirmative, 21; qualified affirmative (Yes, but . . .), 2; negative, 0.

ly, however, they were made to play central roles in a complex social system. Many students volunteered statements saying they had never before fully appreciated the way groups and social forces interacted. Some reported that they had felt the pull of conflicting group loyalties; that they had come to understand a group's point of view by having to argue for, or against it; that they had achieved a better understanding of the complexity of the issues faced by policy makers in a developing country; and that negotiation, bargaining, and the building of political support seemed more real. They also reported that the exercise gave meaning to some of the things they had been reading and discussing in the classroom..

The value of an exercise of this kind depends, in part, on the degree to which the simulate corresponds to the situation simulated. If construction of the game is poor, or the analysis underlying it is in error, then the players are likely to emerge with a distorted view of reality. On the whole, we feel that the Brazilian game corresponded quite well to political life in that country. However, there is room for continuing adjustments in later runs. For example, in the game, political parties emerged as more important and cohesive than they actually are in Brazil. Perhaps, if the party caucus were ruled out in the game, the functioning of political parties would prove to be more realistic. The legislature, when in session, tended to be isolated from the rest of the game, and the members felt too few pressures from their constituents.

In addition, certain distortions related to role playing entered the game. There are three aspects of the role-playing problem that should be distinguished. The first involves inducing players to play their roles as accurately as they can. Players involved in a simulation exercise know it is a "game," and their behavior can hardly fail to be modified, in some way, by that knowledge. How important the behavioral deviation will be, depends on a variety of factors, including the nature of the exercise, the purpose of the experimenters, and the degree of the players' involvement. In the Brazilian exercise, players, even though they knew it was only a game, were deeply involved and took the experience seriously. The more effectively that careful role playing can be made to induce a feeling of distinction and status for a player, the greater will be his incentive to adhere to his role. The design of the Brazilian game might well have given more attention to setting up a system of rewards and punishments aimed at encouraging players to adhere to assigned roles.

The second aspect of the problem is how a player, even assuming he has the best intentions, is to know *how* to play a role. How, for instance, are middle-class American students to cross the culture barrier and play the roles of Brazilian politicians and officials? The problem can be eased somewhat if there is enough time for the players to become socialized into the game and into the conditions of the society being simulated. Since, however, there was not sufficient time for the players to become familiar with their roles and with Brazil, the game suffered. Players, for example, were more compromising than the corresponding personalities on the Brazilian scene would have been. This may have been because the players came out of a tradition that places a higher value on compromise and reasonableness than does the Brazilian, or because their personal interests were not really involved. In any case, even the members of the extreme right wing were inclined toward reformism. In the absence of more data, it is hard to estimate the importance of cross-cultural differences to simulation; nevertheless, the existence of the problem should not be overlooked. We resolved, as a result of that experience, that the next simulation would use players who were more intensively socialized into the game.

The third aspect of the role-playing problem involves the impact upon the game of the personality and value systems of an individual player. In this game, for example, players found it easier to adhere to left wing, rather than right wing roles. The former were probably far more congenial to the type of person who would join the Peace Corps.* Personality factors, such as variations in initiative, aggressiveness, and capacity to become absorbed in the game, are sometimes of central importance. In the Brazilian game, for example, the role of General Kruel was expected to be of only moderate importance. The person cast in this role, however, was a graduate student and a specialist in Latin American affairs who had just returned from a year of research in South America. The night before the game he stayed up late studying the rules and relative strengths of the different groups, and outlining a series of preferred strategies. As soon as the game began, he was able to swing into action, while most of the players were still trying to orient themselves. He played his role with such vigor and initiative that General Kruel became one of the dominant figures in the game.

The importance of these role-playing problems depends on the

---

*Prior to the 1964 election, we polled the trainees, and did not find a single supporter of Senator Goldwater in the group.

purposes of the experimenters and the needs of the players. In the Brazilian exercise, the players obviously got a good deal out of the experience despite the imperfections of the game. They apparently achieved a feeling for the problems of negotiation, policy making, and group interaction in a developing country. They also learned about the economics and politics of Brazil and about the functioning of the country's government. However, they could also receive some false impressions about the way the Brazilian political system works. Post-game analysis, including discussion of the congruence between simulate and the situation simulated, would help minimize this danger.

The problems of role playing are likely to be more serious when man-simulation is used primarily for research purposes. This topic will be discussed in a later chapter.

The Brazilian exercise represented a new approach to the simulation of national systems, since it sought to simulate the processes of an actual country rather than an imaginary country. This experiment carried the use of simulation well beyond the level of Simuland. We emerged confident that future games could be made richer and more complex, provided the players had ample time to familiarize themselves with the game and the country being simulated.

4

SIMULATION OF THE BRAZILIAN POLITICO-ECONOMIC SYSTEM

RULES OF THE GAME

PURPOSE

The purpose of this exercise is to simulate the politico-economic conditions of an actual country—Brazil.

Although important aspects of the structural complexity of Brazil are introduced, the game is designed for players who have no intimate acquaintance with Brazil, and who have had little previous experience with simulation.

TIME SPAN

The game is presumed to begin on January 1, 1965, and to last 3 years. Each hour of the game represents 6 months. In 1967, election year, however, each 6-month period will be 1½ hours long. The game runs for 8 hours, allowing 1 hour for dinner.

The schedule is as follows:

Players will arrive at 1:45 P.M., November 19, in Davie Hall. Game begins at 2:00 P.M.

```
2:00 – 4:00   1965
4:00 – 6:00   1966
6:00 – 7:00   Dinner break
7:00 – 8:30   First 6 months of 1967 (8:30—election)
8:30 –10:00   Second 6 months of 1967
```

THE CONGRESS

The Congress is composed of individuals voted into office in the recent elections. No congressional elections are scheduled during the next 3 years. (Asterisks on the List of Players sheet indicate which players are members of the Congress. The same information appears on the Actor Profile Sheet.)

Congressional sessions are normally 30 minutes in duration.

The Congress is scheduled to meet at the following times: 3:00–3:30; 5:00–5:30; 9:00–9:30.

As indicated in the Constitution, the President may call the Congress into special session. A special session shall not last for more than 15 minutes.

The Presiding Officer (see Actor Profile Sheet) shall call the Congress to order, and begin to conduct the business of the body. For purposes of this game, Robert's *Rules of Order* shall be the accepted procedure for conducting the affairs of Congress. The Congress may alter its procedures and officers by majority vote.

Legislation may be introduced by any member, and may reflect the policy preferences of the government, the individual, his party, or his region.

Decisions shall be by majority vote. In the event of a tie vote, the decision shall be in favor of the side supported by the Presiding Officer.

THE PRESIDENT

The President has a variety of powers and responsibilities in the game. He may dismiss a minister at any time and appoint a successor. He is responsible for the conduct of the foreign policy of Brazil, in both its economic and its political aspects.

He will wish to develop a legislative program in consultation with the Presiding Officer of the Congress, party leaders, and influential persons in the Congress. He may also find it necessary to use his office to influence or assure passage of legislative measures he is interested in.

It is the responsibility of the President to develop an annual Plan for Brazil. (See "The Economy and the Plan.") He may choose to submit the Plan to the Congress for its support, but he need not do so. Development and execution of the budget are executive matters.

The President has a variety of economic powers, such as the right to devalue the cruzeiro. If he is interested in reelection, he will want to begin early in the game to develop support looking toward the election in 1967.

The powers of the President are ill-defined in the Brazilian political system, so if the President is uncertain about a power he wishes to exercise, he should consult with the experimenters.

PRESIDENTIAL ELECTION

A presidential election is scheduled for 1967.

The formation of slates of candidates for President and Vice-President, and the development of electoral support will, therefore, take place between 7:00 and 8:20.

At 8:20, each party or coalition wishing to submit a slate of candidates to the electorate must present this slate to the experimenters. The election will take place at 8:30.

The experimenters will conduct the election by polling the players. Each player will be given a printed ballot containing the competing slates. He will indicate his preference, sign the ballot (with the name of the actor he is playing), and return it to the experimenters.

The experimenters will count the ballots, apply the special weighting for each player, as indicated on the Actor Profile Sheet and List of Players Sheet, and announce the result.

When the result of the election is announced, the new government will take office. The civil servants (Señors Omega and Kappa) remain, but all other elective and appointive officials leave and return to the regions from whence they came (unless the incumbent President is reelected).

Negotiations prior to the election will often concern not only elective officials, but appointive officials as well.

POLITICAL PARTIES

Players may learn their own party affiliations from the Actor Profile Sheet or the List of Players.

Of the numerous parties in Brazil, only the largest have been incorporated into the game.

Party leaders normally take a keen interest in all matters relating to elections, seeing this as the most important way to advance their interests and those of their followers.

They are also likely to take a lively interest in the success or failure of certain pieces of legislation.

THE FOREIGN ENVIRONMENT

For this game, the foreign environment of Brazil contains the following actors: the United States; the World Bank; the Inter-American Development Bank; the International Monetary Fund; Foreign Private Investors; Cuba; the Soviet Union; and Communist China. Of these elements, the United States is, certainly, the most influential. The United States maintains a presence in Brazil in the form of several thousand advisors.

The President is responsible for the conduct of foreign policy. Only the President, his ministers, or civil servants at his direction, can communicate with the external actors.* Various elements in Brazil can, of course, urge the President to take action along certain lines.

Communication between the Brazilian government and the external actors may be initiated by either party.

The IBRD (International Bank for Reconstruction and Development), the IMF, and Inter-American Bank will be played by a single player. The Soviet Union, Communist China, and Cuba will be played by a single player.

In thinking about foreign aid, the foreign actors will pay particular attention to the record of the government in its repayment of previous debt.

PHYSICAL ACTION

Physical action can be taken within the framework of the game. This action includes a broad range of activities extending from peaceful demonstrations to strikes, riots, or a military *coup*.

For any activity in this spectrum, the actor must observe the following procedure:

1. *Statement of intent.* Every actor must serve notice to the experimenters of his purpose, and his proposed physical act. The experimenters will then inform the actor of the earliest time he may initiate action, and the number of stages his activity may take. From the time the initiating actor serves notice, normal negotiations will continue. Also, because of the nature of the activity, the experimenters may inform certain other actors of the impending action, giving them full or partial knowledge according to the realities of Brazilian politics.

---

*Members of the dissident left may communicate with the external Communist actors—Cuba, China, and the Soviet Union.

The initiating actor will be informed as to what information the experimenters released, and to whom it was released.

2. The initiating actor informs the experimenters, after the imposed waiting period has passed, that he has initiated the first stage. The experimenters then poll those actors who might influence the action and announce the factual outcome. At this time, the experimenters also inform the initiating actor of the earliest moment that he can initiate the second stage if he wishes to continue.

3. Again, after the deadline, the initiating actor informs the experimenters that he has taken the action. Once again the experimenters poll relevant players and announce the result.

4. The experimenters may impose limits on the number of physical action sequences that will be allowed in the game.

COMMUNICATIONS

Players may communicate orally with other players in their region.

They may communicate by phone with individuals in other regions if those persons are members of the same political party, or if they fall into the same category in the Government Plan.

All phone conversations are to be limited to two minutes. The telephone operator is under instruction to disconnect all conversations of greater length.

Physical movement is restricted in the game. Players cannot leave their region except under the following conditions:

The President and his minister have free movement throughout the country. He may call any player to his office. A player cannot go to see the President without an invitation.

All governors have free physical movement.

Legislators may leave their regions to go to meetings of the Congress.

Military personnel may congregate at the military club at any time.

All other communication shall be by written message. Any player may communicate with any other player via written message.

Messages and manifestoes may be issued jointly.

Periodically, *The Brazilian News* will be published and distributed to all players. Players wishing to make press releases should address them to the newspaper, making the communication as brief as possible.

Stories appearing in the *Brazilian News* and originating with the Associated Press may be treated as *fact*, for the purposes of the game. (These will normally be dispatches from the experimenters, communicating developments during the game.)

The experimenters may also use the facilities of Radio Brazil (public address system or bull horn) for speedy communication with actors. Information communicated over the radio by the "experimenters" may be treated as fact.

REPORTING

If the lessons of a simulation exercise are to be learned, and if the game is to be improved, it is essential that a careful record be kept of developments during the game.

Members of the reporting team will observe the game and will try to be alert to all matters relating to the content of the game (strategy, tactics, the thinking underlying decisions, etc.) and to its conduct. They will be free to circulate among players, asking questions for clarification where necessary. They will take care, of course, not to interfere with the conduct of the game.

The reporting team will: (1) Maintain a chronology of events in the game, keeping it as nearly up to date as possible at all times; (2) maintain a running description and analysis of what is happening in the game, and why; and (3) participate with the experimenters in a post-game evaluation session, the basis of which will be the account of the game mentioned immediately above.

THE EXPERIMENTERS

The experimenters, at their discretion, may introduce new factors into the game. These variables might concern the external environment of Brazil or its internal affairs.

For purposes of control, the experimenters are to be informed, by the President or an agent of his, of all major governmental decisions and actions.

In the event any player is uncertain about the permissibility of a projected line of action, he should consult with the experimenters. The experimenters may choose to disallow any action that does not seem to them to be in keeping with the purposes of the game.

ACTOR ROLE PLAYING

Individual players will find roles assigned on the sheet entitled "The Players."

THE PLAYERS

The distribution of players in each region is intended to correspond to the social, political, and economic realities of that region, some elements being more heavily weighted than others.

The Players	Voting Strength
The government	
His Excellency Castelo Branco, President of Brazil, UDN	1
Señor Roberto Campos, Minister of Planning, PSD	1
Señor Gouveia de Bulhões, Minister of Finance, UDN	1
General Psi, Director, Northeast Development Authority (SUDENE), UDN	1
*Señor Omega, governmental staff, UDN	2
*Señor Kappa, civil servant, Development Administration, PSD	3
Guanabara	
Governor Carlos Lacerda, UDN	1
General Alpha, Commanding Officer, 1st Army, PSD	1
General Beta, PTB	1
*Señor Gamma, labor leader, PTB	6
*Señor Delta, urban middle-class politician, PSD	3
Minas Gerais	
Governor Pinto, UDN	1
*Señor Epsilon, member of the landed gentry, PSD	3
Señor Zeta, member of the landed gentry, PSD	3
*Señor Eta, intellectual, PSB	6
*Señor Theta, mining interests, PSD	1
Rio Grande do Sul	
General Iota, Commanding Officer, Third Army, UDN	1
*Bishop Mitre, PDC	1
Señor Kappa, labor leader, PTB	3
Señor Mu, landed gentry, PSD	1
*Señor Lambda, urban middle class, UDN	3
States of the Interior	
*Señor Nu, wood products developer, PTB	1
*Señor Xi, cattle, Presiding Officer of the Legislature, UDN	4
Northeast	
*Señor Omicron, landed gentry, cotton, PSD	1
Señor Pi, landed gentry, cacao, PTB	1

(continued)

THE PLAYERS (Cont.)

The Players	Voting Strength
Monsignor Rho, Catholic leader, UDN	4
Señor Sigma, Peasant League leader, PTB	15
São Paulo	
Governor Ademar de Barros, PSP	1
General Kruel, 2nd Army, PSD	1
Señor Tau, industrialist, UDN	2
*Señor Upsilon, industrialist, PSP	2
Señor Phi, labor leader, PTB	10
*Señor Chi, urban middle class, PSP	10
Señor Cuppa, coffee exporter, PSD	3

Foreign actors

There are eight foreign actors.

(A) 1. International Bank for Reconstruction and Development
       2. International Monetary Fund
       3. Inter-American Development Bank
(B) 4. Soviet Union
       5. Communist China
       6. Cuba
(C) 7. United States
       8. Foreign private investors

*Member of the legislature.

The role for each player will be defined on the Actor Profile Sheet. This sheet will indicate party affiliation, voting weight in the general election, and the position of the player on current issues. These issues are discussed in the section "Current Issues in Brazil."

Economic interests of actors are described, in summary form, on the sheet "Economic Roles of Selected Actors."

Players should be guided by the positions ascribed, but they need not feel completely bound. A player might change his position on an issue, as a consequence of changed circumstances or opportunistic advantage, and still remain faithful to the broad interests and attitudes of the individual whose role is being played. In the event of a *coup* or a change of government following the elections, a player might need to rethink his position on some of the issues.

The success of the exercise depends upon the ability of the players to adhere to assigned roles. If the experimenters believe that a player is significantly out of character, they will ask him to justify his behavior. If he cannot do so to their satisfaction, they will reprimand him.

THE ECONOMY AND THE PLAN

Economic Roles of Selected Actors. A number of actors in the game have distinct economic roles. Their interests, primary and secondary, are set forth in the page entitled "The Economic Roles of Selected Actors," which immediately precedes this section. The meaning of "primary and "secondary" interests, and the game procedures to realize them, will be made clear below.

The Government Plan. (A sample Government Plan form, with its 6 categories, is included immediately following this section on the economy.) The development of the Plan is central to the operation of the game. Associated with Categories I and II in the Plan are players whose broad economic interests center on the sector of the economy corresponding to each of these categories. The players whose primary interests fall within a given category will normally work together to obtain for their category as large an allocation of government funds (set forth in the Plan) as possible. Players from the Northeast and States of the Interior, for example, will try to maximize the allocation to Category I.

While the players having a common primary interest can agree on the importance of having a large allocation to that category, their interests are, nevertheless, not completely homogeneous. Six players may be interested in Category I, but one may be interested in irrigation,

ACTOR PROFILE

     I.   Name and title of actor _____

    II.   Region _____

   III. Party affiliation _____

  IV. Voting weight in general election _____

    V.   Member of the legislature? (yes or no) _____

  VI. Description of functional role _____

 VII. Actor interests: primary _____ secondary _____

VIII. Position on selected politico-economic issues:

    A. *Land reform*
       1. Total opposition to any reform _____
       2. Tax penalty on unused land _____
       3. Expropriation with payment in long-term bonds, not adjusted for inflation, for all land over 200 hectares _____

    B. *Inflation versus austerity*
       1. Favors extreme inflation _____
       2. Favors mild inflation _____
       3. Favors austerity _____

    C. *Foreign aid and foreign investment versus economic nationalism*
       1. Favors aid and investment by both U.S. and international organizations _____
       2. Favors foreign aid but with nationalist protection and no strings _____
       3. Opposes further foreign aid and foreign investment and favors expropriation of foreign holdings _____

    D. *Presidential powers*
       1. Favors states rights, anti-centralist position _____
       2. Favors a stronger legislature vis-à-vis President _____
       3. Favors centralization and an increase in presidential powers as a means of achieving national goals _____
       4. Opportunistic, depending on nature of government in power _____

    E. *Welfare*
       1. Favors extension of welfare benefits _____
       2. Opposes extension of welfare benefits _____

    F. *Role of the military in Brazilian politics*
       1. Favors a narrowly professional military _____
       2. Believes military should play role as arbiter of Constitution and balancing force _____
       3. Favors a continuing and active role for military in Brazilian politics _____

ECONOMIC ROLES OF SELECTED ACTORS

I.   Domestic Actors with Primary Interests and Secondary Interests in Plan Categories I-II (References are to Category and Item Number in Government Plan)

	Interests	
Actors and Brief Description	*Primary*	*Secondary*
I. 1. Omicron: Landed gentry, cotton, Northeast	I, 1	II, 5; I, 5
2. Sigma: Peasant leader, Northeast	I, 2	I, 1
3. Xi: Landed gentry, cattle, Mato Grosso (Interior)	I, 3	I, 4
4. Nu: Developer of wood products, Amazonas (Interior)	I, 4	I, 3
5. Pi: Landed gentry, cacao, Northeast	I, 5	I, 1
6. Rho: anti-Communist Catholic leader, Northeast	I, 6	I, 2
II. 1. Tau: Automobile manufacturer, São Paulo	II, 1	II, 7; II, 8
2. Theta: Iron mining magnate, Minas Gerais	II, 2	II, 8
3. Gamma: Labor leader, Guanabara	II, 3	II, 9; II, 10
4. Mu: Landed gentry, sheep, Rio Grande do Sul	II, 4	I, 3
5. Epsilon: Landed gentry, cotton, Minas Gerais	II, 5	I, 1
6. Cuppa: Landed gentry, coffee exporter, São Paulo	II, 6	II, 5
7. Zeta: Landed gentry and mining magnate, Minas Gerais	II, 7	II, 5; II, 2
8. Upsilon: Chemical manufacturer, São Paulo	II, 8	II, 1;
9. Kappa: Labor leader, Rio Grande do Sul	II, 9	II, 10
10. Phi: Labor leader, São Paulo	II, 10	II, 9

a second in welfare, and a third in transportation. Because of the difference in specific interests, players will have varying ideas concerning the way available funds should be spent. Therefore, players who have a *common* interest in getting as large an allocation as possible from the Plan *to* a given category will, nevertheless, compete among themselves for the allocation of funds *within* that category.

In addition to a primary interest, each actor has a secondary interest, which overlaps the primary interest of another actor. These secondary interests suggest some of the natural lines of alliance among players.

Since government income is rarely sufficient to cover the planned allocation of funds, it is not enough for an economic player to concern himself with the proposed allocation to a sector and the division within a sector; he must also compete for the *actual* expenditure of funds. (See "Planned" and "Actual" expenditure in Plan.)

The "satisfaction level" of a player indicates the minimum allocation by the government to his primary interest that he will consider acceptable. Because of limited resources and the extent of the demands made on the government, allocations to a number of actors are likely to fall below this level. (See "Actor Satisfaction Level" in Plan.)

When minimum satisfaction levels are not met, actors adversely affected may wish to consider the avenues of political action that may be open to them. Governors and legislators, for example, will normally be sensitive to the political and economic wants of powerful figures in their region. Economic satisfaction or dissatisfaction will also have an effect on the outcome of an election, and may, therefore, figure in negotiations prior to the election.

Members of the bureaucracy and the military will exert political and other pressures to maintain their present high levels of satisfaction in Categories III and IV.

The government normally tries to maintain the allocation in category VI, "Development Plan," since high levels of expenditure here speed up the overall development of the economy. However, pressure from actors may lead to a diversion of funds from this category, to the detriment of coordinated economic growth.

Foreign actors are likely to pay particular attention to Category V, "Repayment of Foreign Debt." Failure to meet the minimum satisfaction levels of foreign actors may prejudice the receipt of further foreign aid.

The Government Income. (A sample Government Income form is included after the Government Plan.) An estimate of expected income will be one of the President's major considerations in the construction of the Government Plan. The bulk of government income derives from taxes and returns on government investment. The experimenters will inform the government, at the beginning of the budgetary cycle, of the estimated government income from these sources. They will inform the government of the actual income half-way through the cycle.

The amount of foreign aid available will depend on the success of the government in soliciting funds for government programs and attracting investment in private industry. Foreign actors may attach stipulations to whatever aid they may give or whatever investment they may make. The stipulations may be political in nature, or may specify that the funds be used in a particular sector of the economy.

Income from all sources is usually insufficient to meet planned allocations. In these circumstances, the government often resorts to the printing of money. Because government income is insufficient to meet planned allocations, government and actors are forced into a 2-step negotiation: first, negotiation of *planned* government allocations to categories and to primary interests; second, negotiation prior to *actual* expenditure of funds on actors' primary interests. The second step may or may not follow the Plan, and will involve government distribution of "Confirmation of Expenditure" sheets.

Inflation. Inflation is a constant factor in the Brazilian economy. It involves an increase in the supply of money, and a decline in the purchasing power of the unit of exchange. Therefore, inflation leads not only to an increase in the minimum satisfaction levels of individual actors, but also to demands on the government for correspondingly increased allocations in the Plan. These demands may be met out of government income, which will increase at approximately the same inflationary rate.

The impact of inflation is not uniform on all actors, however. If an actor's minimum satisfaction level has risen by a percentage which is *less* than the "average rate of inflation, or national norm over last year," his position will have improved in real terms. Conversely, if an actor's minimum satisfaction level rises by a percentage which is *more* than that of the national norm, he will be placed at a disadvantage. An actor's dissatisfaction with the relative impact of inflation upon him may be alleviated by a promise of a generous government allocation for the following year. Failing this, he may choose to resort to political action as a means of protest.

Neither the government nor individual players can anticipate the exact magnitude of inflation in a given year, but both will be given an estimated inflationary increase by the experimenters. This estimate will be used in preliminary negotiations for the Government Plan which will apply in the next year. Actors and the government will negotiate allocations for the following year on the basis of their estimated new satisfaction levels and anticipated government income.

At the end of *each* period, the experimenters will distribute new copies of blank Government Plans with the new actor-satisfaction levels on them.*

---

*The experimenters found it helpful to prepare several sets of scaled satisfaction levels before the game began. Then, instead of having to compute new satisfaction levels under pressure during the game, they were able to select from among existing scales the one that best suited the situation that had emerged.

THE GOVERNMENT PLAN

Tentative Category Plan _____   Year _____
Final Government Plan _____
Final Annual Expenditure Report _____

Real average rate of inflation over last year used in computing new levels of satisfaction here: _____

Primary Actors	Primary Economic Interests	Actor Satis- faction Level	Expenditure	
			Planned	Actual

Category I. Regional development, the Northeast and the States of the Interior

Omicron	(1) Irrigation in the Northeast	25		
Sigma	(2) Lower class welfare, Northeast	10		
Xi	(3) Transportation development, Interior	10		
Nu	(4) Aid to new industry, Interior	10		
Pi	(5) Keep high exchange rate, ex- ports	30		
Rho	(6) Credit for small farmers	25		
	Category Total:	110		

Category II. Regional development, the Central and Southern States

Tau	(1) Electricity, São Paulo	60		
Theta	(2) Transportation, Minas Gerais	50		
Gamma	(3) Housing and schools, Guanabara	25		
Mu	(4) Livestock research, Rio Grande do Sul	10		
Epsilon	(5) Research on crop improvement	15		
Cuppa	(6) No required coffee sales to Government	15		
Zeta	(7) End price controls	10		
Upsilon	(8) Tax incentives for retooling	10		
Kappa	(9) Wage raises and urban welfare	20		
Phi	(10) Lower food price in cities	40		
	Category Total:	255		

THE GOVERNMENT PLAN (Cont.)

Primary Actors	Primary Economic Interests	Actor Satis- faction Level	Expenditure	
			Planned	*Actual*

Category III. Military expenditure

All military personnel

Category Total: 175

Category IV. Government salaries and operations

Bureaucrats

Category Total: 75

Category V. Repayment of foreign debt

Foreign Actors

Category Total: 73

Category VI. Development plan

All Actors

Category Total: 75

Grand Total: 763

Expected average rate of inflation, or national norm, for next year (% increase in satisfaction levels for negotiation on next year's plan). _____

THE GOVERNMENT INCOME

Tentative:
Final: Year: _____

Sources	Expected	Actual
(1) Taxes and return from Government investment		
(2) Foreign aid from actor (1) stipulations:		
(3) Foreign aid from actor (2) stipulations:		
(4) Foreign aid from actor (3) stipulations:		
(5) Money printed to meet necessary expenditures		
Totals:		

FLOW SHEET

2:00

(1) Tentative category plan, 1965* (planned expenditure to categories only filled in).
(2) Expected average rate of inflation for next year, 1966.

2:45

Experimenters give government real revenue from taxes and return from government investment for 1965.

2:00

Actors will have their own plan record sheet titled "The Government Plan."

Actors whose interests fall in a given category negotiate on the adequacy of the government's planned expenditure to their category as measured by their joint satisfaction levels. Foreign actors negotiate on the basis of planned expenditure to the repayment of foreign debt and/or other allocations of interest to them.

All actors also negotiate planned expenditure to their primary interests and, if possible, to their secondary interests.

3:00

(1) Final government plan, 1965 with planned expenditure to primary interests filled in).
(2) Tentative government income, 1965.

3:00

Legislature meets until 3:30.

Actors press for actual expenditures. Those dissatisfied with the plan may seek payment beyond the planned expenditure. Government consideration of 1966 plan will begin. Actors may bargain for proportionately greater allocations next year.

3:30

(1) Foreign actors give the government the final amount of foreign aid for 1965.
(2) Actors get new plan record Sheet with real rate of inflation and new actor satisfaction levels.
(3) Experimenters give government expected income from taxes and return for next year, 1966.

3:30

Actors should attempt to get Certificates of Government Expenditure by this time.

---

*For the purposes of the game, the government has been given a sample plan and the expected revenue figure for 1965.

FLOW SHEET (Cont.)

4:00
(1) Final annual expenditure report, 1965 (actual expenditure to primary interests recorded).
(2) Total government income for 1965 (including total money printed).
(3) Tentative category plan, 1966.
(4) Expected average rate of inflation for next year, 1967

4:00
Actors negotiate on category expenditure.

4:45
Experimenters give government real tax and return for 1966 (as adjusted for inflation).

4:45
Actors negotiate on expenditure to primary interests.

5:00
(1) Final government plan, 1966.
(2) tentative government income, 1966.

5:00
Legislature meets until 5:30.

Actors press for actual expenditure.

5:30
(1) Foreign actors give final aid figure.
(2) Experimenters give real effects of inflation and new plan record sheet.
(3) Experimenters give government expected income from taxes and return for next year, 1967.

5:30
Actors should attempt to have certificates by this time.

6:00
Final annual expenditure report, 1966.

DINNER

7:00
(1) Tentative category plan, 1967.

7:00
Actors negotiate on category expenditure.

FLOW SHEET (Cont.)

(2) Expected average rate of inflation for next year, 1967.

Actors negotiate on expenditure
to primary interests.

7:45
Experimenters give government
real revenue from taxes and return for 1967 (as adjusted for
inflation).

8:00
Final government plan, 1967.

8:00
Election period begins.
Actors press for actual expendi-
ture and *keep pressing*.

8:20
All candidate slates are due.

8:30
Election.

8:45
Election results announced and
elected government takes office.

9:30
Foreign actors give final aid
figure.

9:30
Actors should attempt to have
certificates.

10:00
Final annual expenditure report,
1967.

THE BRAZILIAN POLITICAL SYSTEM

THE MILITARY

In Brazil, the military is a key political force, in that it establishes limits within which the political behavior of other groups is constrained and confined. The military, when it chooses to be, is a major decision-making force on matters of governmental policy and constitutionalism. However, it can establish the limits of civilian political behavior only when it is able to develop an internal consensus. The occasions on which the military feels called upon to make major political decisions are relatively few, and most frequently relate to the question of who is to occupy the office of President. Even its most recently approved President—Castelo Branco who is a General himself—is subject to continuing surveillance by the military. During the last 2 years, the military has given signs of departing from its previous practice of interesting itself only in questions of major import and has, on occasion, intervened in lesser questions

When a crisis occurs, the military commanders assemble, usually in the "Military Club," and, in effect, take a vote on the matter to be decided. Prior to this meeting, they engage in "campaigns" to win support from within the military services for their various points of view. These campaigns involve bargaining among Generals and Admirals according to their influence and reflect the professional prestige, official position, and the forces these military men command. Before the recent revolution, this search for political support within the military extended to the enlisted ranks. Another factor of great importance in negotiations is inter-personal relationships —friendships, animosities, and family ties—among military commanders.

Intervention of the military in politics rests on the basis not only of military power, but also of the Constitution, which states: "It is the mission of the armed forces to defend the country and guarantee the constitutional powers, law and order." With the sanction of this provision, the military, once it agrees internally on a course of action, can do anything it chooses, so long as it acts under the guise of preserving the "constitutional powers." In April of 1964, for example, the military leadership deposed the President, and decreed an "Institutional Act" amending the Constitution of 1946. This act provided that the commanders-in-chief of the 3 armed services could oust any federal, state, or municipal official, including any elected member of the legislature, whom they considered to be "extremist"; they could suspend political rights (voting and holding office) for 10 years and suspend the immunity of any judge, professor, or other officeholder, for 6 months. In addition, it empowered the President to send to the Congress legislation which would have to be acted on within 30 days; if not acted on, it would become law forthwith.

REGIONAL POLITICS

Brazil also has its own distinctive patterns of regional politics and economic interests. While Amazônia is sparsely populated, it obtains many concessions, because its votes in the Congress are needed by the major actors; these can be traded off, as in the case of a special program established for the economic development of the area. The Northeast is politically significant because of the growing threat posed by the organized Peasant Leagues of Francisco Julião and others; because of the problems of drought and poverty (unrest is rife, and tends to spread to other areas when nothing is done to alleviate conditions); and because of the growing economic importance of the region in the production of sugar cane, cacao, and, most recently, oil. Minas Gerais lies athwart the Rio-Brasília communication route, and has a strong economy in mining and agriculture. It has a very large population, and, unlike Amazônia and the Northeast, a strong entrepreneurial group. Rio de Janeiro is populous, the national tourist center, a hotbed of urban social problems, the headquarters of a large military establishment, and the "real" capital of the country. It is the prestige residential spot of Brazil, and the locus of most political communication on national matters. São Paulo is the major industrial region, the center of the industrial and commercial elite and of technological advancement. It has more internal political discipline than any other state. Rio Grande do Sul has a strong economy based on cattle and agriculture, as well as scattered local industries (silver, leather, processing of agricultural products). It is sufficiently isolated for the military there to be independent.

The regions are culturally distinct, as well. Rio Grande do Sul, though predominantly European, is non-Iberian (German and Italian). São Paulo is mixed European. Rio is cosmopolitan; strongly Portuguese, but with an admixture of Negro and mestizo populations. The Northeast is Portuguese in its elite, heavily Negro in the coastal populated area, and mestizo in the backlands. Amazônia is predominantly mestizo. From south to north, the educational level grows progressively lower, markedly so, north of Rio. The same holds true as we move from coast to hinterland.

These diversities dominate relationships among regional politicians. The ties of party or coalition are transient compared with those of region. Communication among elites within a region is considerable. Among members of a single elite (landed gentry, intellectuals, military, etc.) in different regions, communication is not quite as good. The most effective elite communication networks, nationally speaking, are probably possessed by the military, the entrepreneurial elite of the major cities, and the landed gentry (who tend to reside in the cities), in that order. Other elites communicate less.

POLITICAL PARTIES

There are 13 political parties in Brazil, each with greatly varying characteristics. The large parties are most diverse in their makeup and are non-ideological in their orientation. They are largely reflections of their current leaders. Some of the smaller parties are ideological in orientation. The parties are briefly characterized as follows:

Social Democratic Party (118). * The chief aim of the PSD is to stay in power. It has no other goals. It was the party of the President until 1960, chiefly by virtue of its alliance with the—

Brazilian Labor Party (114). The PTB is reform oriented, but is not, strictly speaking, a labor party, even though its leader became President, and was the dominant figure in the labor movement. Especially in the north, many intellectuals and men of wealth are members of the party. The PTB is needed by the PSD to stay in power. Under Goulart, the alliance continued.

National Democratic Union (94). The UDN was for a long time prior to the revolution, the major opposition party; it opposed Vargas and his heirs. Though it tends to be rightist, it has a reform wing. With the revolution, it became much stronger, by virtue of the suppression of the leaders of PTB and PSD who were closely associated with the Goulart administration. A leading candidate for the next presidential election and Castelo Branco belong to this party.

Social Progress Party (23). This party is under the strong leadership of Ademar de Barros, the state "boss" of São Paulo. The PSP tends to cooperate with the UDN on political matters.

*This figure, given for each party, is the number of seats held by that party in the lower chamber of the Brazilian Congress in September of 1964, and is a rough indication of the strength and importance of the parties.

Christian Democratic Party (16). The PDC is ideological in nature, combining democratic, Christian, and socialist beliefs into its program and social policy.

National Labor Party (12). This party is, in essential respects, similar in ideology to the Christian Democratic Party, and is an offshoot of the PTB. It originally intended to form a "true" labor party.

All Other Parties (9). The Communist Party is outlawed; it would constitute the fourteenth party, if legalized. It has operated through other parties such as the PTB and Brazilian Socialist Party.

Political parties in Brazil do not have a high degree of internal organization, as they are, in fact, systems constituted by the rural *coronel* and the urban *chefe politico.* These political figures will adhere to a particular political party as it suits their interests, shifting from party to party when they see advantage in doing so. Often, they will come together in coalitions in order to capture the machinery of the state governments. Thus, each state government rests on a division of spoils among 2 or 3 parties, each consisting of a set of bosses. The tie of constituent to boss is the strongest nexus. Next to that is the tie of boss to his region or state. Regardless of party, politicians of a particular region will normally join together to get the most they can from the central government or the national parties. States like Minas Gerais, São Paulo, and Rio Grande do Sul are strong political entities in themselves, but in other areas where the states are weaker politically there is a tendency for the states to band together in a regional coalition to obtain funds and other advantages from the national government. The Northeast and "Amazônia" are notable examples.

In general, "confusion is endemic to the system."*

STRUCTURES OF GOVERNMENT

The President is chosen by direct popular election for a 5-year term. There has long been a tradition of a strong executive in Brazil, and the informal power of the President is considerable. His formal powers include those legal privileges normally ascribed to the chief of state, such as the power to appoint ministers of state and other officials. Notably exempt from the President's powers are the armed forces, of which he is only in nominal command. Because of the need

*Phyllis Petersen, "Brazil: Institutionalized Confusion," *Political Systems of Latin America*, ed. by Martin C. Needler (D. Van Nostrand Company, Princeton, N. J., 1964), p. 483. This selection is a concise analysis of Brazil, perhaps the best single source that can be recommended to players. We found it highly valuable in constructing the game.

to build coalitions to win the national election, the Vice-President, elected by a separate ballot, is usually not of the same party as the President. Most presidents come from the more powerful states, generally Minas Gerais and São Paulo, and, in two cases, from Rio Grande do Sul. President Branco, an exception to this rule, is a native of Ceara in the Northeast.

Elections for the National Congress are held every 4 years. The Chamber of Deputies is constituted by proportional representation, and Senators are chosen for 8-year terms by direct, plurality election. The Congress is weighted in the direction of the landed gentry, especially the Senate, in which the small states have equal strength. Hence, the Congress has a conservative cast, though it has every shade of opinion represented, including that of the Communists, who work underground. In general, the President and Congress have been able to cooperate (especially since all benefits flow from dispensations of the President); however, it has not been so since the regimes of Jânio Quadros, the reformer, and Goulart, his successor. Both Goulart and Quadros sought to increase their power at the expense of the Congress, in order, it is presumed, to carry out reforms. Since Congress would not go along with the Goulart program, the 1962 elections were sharply fought on this issue. To some extent, Goulart's supporters gained in this election. With the revolution, however, the President, representing the Revolutionary Command, removed 40 deputies from the lower chamber, and replaced them with defeated candidates in the previous election. This change produced a much more conservative Congress, even though the party distribution did not change substantially. The President's relations with the Congress remain essentially personal, rather than politically partisan in nature.

RECENT POLITICAL HISTORY IN BRAZIL

In early February, 1961, Jânio Quadros became President of Brazil after the greatest electoral performance in the history of the country; he defeated his opponent, General Lott, by a margin of over 2,000,000 votes. He was swept into office on a program more explicit in social and governmental reform than had ever been the case before. While Vargas had talked like a reformer in his early days, his administration, after enacting some advanced social security and labor legislation, took a conservative turn.

Quadros was prepared to wage an all-out attack on the massive problems of corruption and inefficiency in government. The extent of his political support in the election is more remarkable when it is considered that he virtually repudiated partisan support, including that of his own party, the conservative União Democrática Nacional. Indeed, his was a personal victory. After inauguration, however, in attempting to carry out a series of reforms, he was opposed at every turn by vested interests in and out of government.

In addition to his domestic reform policy, he charted a new course in foreign policy, termed the "Independent" foreign policy. This meant independence from the United States (influenced by a strong dose of anti-Americanism) and other major powers. Quadros made friendly overtures to the Communist countries, most notably, Cuba. This earned the enmity of the armed forces with whom Quadros had never come to an "understanding," contrary to one of the basic rules of Brazilian politics. Evidently he felt that since he was the champion of the people, the usual institutional support of party, military, and some of the elites was unnecessary. Moreover, Quadros was an idealist, and somewhat unstable emotionally. These factors created an untenable situation, and demonstrated that even a "popular hero" must observe the political "rules of the game."

Quadros' response to this situation was to resign his job on August 25, 1961, 7 months after his election. It seems clear that his reason for doing so was to create a situation in which the masses would pour into the streets in a demonstration of support for him, and somehow vanquish his various internal and foreign enemies. There was no demonstration, and Quadros, in disappointment, flew to London.

João Goulart, who as Vice-President was the successor to Quadros under the Constitution, was then abroad visiting chiefly the Communist countries. Goulart was the leader of the second largest party in Brazil, the Partido Trabalhista Brasileiro, and the protegé of Vargas who had originally organized the party. Goulart had a strong leftist image, despite being a large landholder in Rio Grande do Sul. In the international arena, at least, he appeared to be pro-Communist. He did not have the confidence of the military forces, with the exception of the large Third Army, stationed in his home state of Rio Grande do Sul in Southern Brazil—the land of the gaúcho nationalists.

For a week, the great question was whether the military would permit Goulart to assume office. The Air Force controlled the airfields of the country through which Goulart would have to return to the country. Whatever the internal politics of the military may have been, the usual process in any political crisis took place; namely, an intense series of conferences among the military chieftains. The strong and vocal support (including promises to fight in support of Goulart) of the Third Army leaders prevailed, and the decision was reached to permit Goulart to occupy the presidency. This was regarded as a great victory for constitutionalism within Brazil at the time.

In the process, however, the anti-Goulart faction exacted what they thought was a heavy price. Goulart was stripped of many of the normal presidential powers by an amendment to the Constitution called the "Additional Act" (the Constitution being the post-Vargas document dating from 1946); this amendment established a "parliamentary system" with a President of a Council of Ministers, his Council serving as a parliamentary cabinet. Thus, the executive power was split in a rather vague fashion between the President and the President of the Council of Ministers.

Since in practice, however, it was Goulart who appointed the President of the Council of Ministers, from that moment he dominated the affairs of government. Nevertheless, Goulart adopted the strategy of increasing his powers by asserting that he could not carry out his reform program (agrarian, tax, administrative, and urban reform) without a restoration of his full powers. His first 1½ years in office were spent in a campaign to repeal the Additional Act and redeem the presidential system. During this time, Brazil's troubles increased in the economic and administrative spheres to such a degree that some credence was lent to Goulart's assertions that he could not govern effectively with limited powers. From here on, there was little opposition to his campaign for repeal; in the referendum, held on January 6, 1963, the Additional Act was abolished by a vote in the ratio of 5 to 1.

Brazil's financial crisis, reflected in a devastating rate of inflation, had continued to deepen. In September of 1962 Goulart had initiated a national economic development plan, known as the "Plano Trienal," aimed at solving his, and some of Brazil's, problems. Not only was this plan appealing to him and fitting to his program of reform, it was also being urged on him by all the international lending agencies and the United States government as a condition for gaining new aid and the refunding of existing loans. In a crash program between September and January (stimulated in part by the hope that the birth of "the Plan" would help in the plebiscite of January 6), a newly appointed Minister of Planning, Celso Furtado, an economist, produced a plan which was based chiefly on research done over a number of years by various groups of economists, including missions from the United States and the United Nations Economic Commission for Latin America. Goulart promulgated the Plan on New Year's Day, before the plebiscite, and committed himself fully to its implementation.

Three months later, he fired the Minister of Planning and the Finance Minister (an eminent left-wing professor named San Tiago Dantas), and repudiated the Plan publicly. This "about face" is not difficult to explain. The Plan, as promulgated, required belt tightening and closer relations with the United States and the International Monetary Fund. The leftist groups in the country—consisting of the Communists (now illegal as a party), the radical anti-imperialist nationalists, the National Students' Union, a left-wing element in the military (especially among the NCO's and junior officers), and a number of far-left federal deputies—opposed both requirements of the Plan. The nationalist Communist types presumed that increased United States aid and closer ties were dangers. Organized labor was fearful of the prospect of austerity (such as a limit of 40 per cent on salary increases when they had demanded 70 per cent in an inflationary situation). These groups established a tight coalition. Since they had constituted the backbone of Goulart's support, their refusal to go along with the Plano Trienal forced Goulart to abandon it and repudiate the foreign support he had sought. As a consequence of this repudiation, the industrial and commercial community became as worried about Goulart as the military already were, perceiving his actions as a move to the left (despite an original suspicion that the Plano Trienal itself was a socialist document). This situation led to a widening of the breach between the pro- and anti-Goulart forces, a situation that led ultimately to the revolution which ousted Goulart.

By March, 1964, President Goulart was prepared to push his "reform" program which emphasized strengthening the presidency. By now, many feared that he intended to take over as a dictator, abolish elections, and perpetrate a "Vargian" *coup*. He scheduled a mass meeting for the 13th (Friday) of March. At this meeting, he demanded progress on "reforms" including establishment of diplomatic relations with Communist China, legalization of the Brazilian Communist Party, extension of the suffrage to illiterates (with whom only the Goulard forces had ties) and to enlisted men in the military forces (where the leftists had made great gains), payment in bonds (instead of cash) for lands confiscated by the government for agrarian reform, and creation of a whole new group of rural labor unions. The meeting was a success, causing the moderates and non-Communists to become seriously worried.

Certain military and civilian leaders apparently began making plans at this point, fearing a Castro type of regime. Then an event undermined the basis of military power itself: The marines, in a demonstration of solidarity with the program of the leftist coalition and the President, were insubordinate to their military superiors; the President promptly granted an amnesty to all of the mutineers. With this threat before them, the leaders of the prospective revolution hastened to make their plans final.

On March 31, the Governor of Minas Gerais announced the revolution. He had previously won the support of the leading civilian and military leaders in Minas Gerais, São Paulo, and Guanabara, an almost invincible combination, since it included 2 of the 3 major armies in the nation and the industrial center of the country. After a few days of uncertainty, in which a few forces in Rio and Rio Grande do Sul remained loyal to the government, the bloodless revolution was a complete success. Goulart fled the country, thus resigning his position as President under the Constitution.

The military-civilian coalition named Castelo Branco, a career general with no strong political ties, to the presidency. He was the compromise candidate of the moderates and the radical right.

During the next 6 months, a purge occurred in which several hundred Brazilians were stripped of their political rights because of "subversive" connections with the ousted regime. Many of these individuals have either fled the country or submerged themselves into a Communist-oriented underground.

While there have been no executions, some critics of the regime argue that it has been too harsh in its punishment of Goulart associates. Others hold that the regime has not been harsh enough. Supporters of the latter point of view appear to be opposed to any substantial reforms. Those of the former persuasion seem to agree with Castelo Branco that a moderate program of reform, including agrarian reform, must take place.

The Brazilian economy still flounders; basic problems remain unsolved, while rightist and centrist groups jockey for power. The current fear is of another *coup* that may move the country further to the right.

ECONOMIC DESCRIPTION

Brazil is a country of economic extremes. The regions indicated on the map (Fig. 1) as Northeast and the States of the Interior are primarily producers of agricultural products and raw materials, and have been virtually untouched by the industrial revolution. Methods of production and patterns of land handling in these regions have not changed much in the last 50 years, even though some goods from these regions are exported. In contrast, the regions of Minas Gerais, São Paulo, Rio Grande do Sul, and Guanabara (the central and southern states) have experienced substantial economic development. In each of these regions, there are large modern industrial complexes, particularly in the cities. The central and southern states also produce

Figure 1. Population and Produce by region. Population: light. 1; moderate, 2, 3, 6; dense, 4, 5, (and cities in other regions). Produce: cotton, 2, 3; coffee, 5, 6; sugar 2 (along coast); livestock, 6, 2, 1; mining, 3, 1; manufacturing 5, 4, 6, 3.

agricultural products and raw materials, but production of these goods involves modern methods, and the area, considered as a whole, is wealthier. Our discussion of the economy of Brazil will concentrate first on the development of the Northeast and States of the Interior and then on the development of the central and southern states. We will then consider topics of major importance in the economic life of the country.

I. REGIONAL DEVELOPMENT: THE NORTHEAST AND THE STATES OF THE INTERIOR

The Northeast. While the Northeast has long been a producer of sugar and cacao for export, the wealth created by these exports has done little to raise the general welfare of the area's population. In recent decades, the foreign exchange earned by exports from the Northeast have actually gone to foster the prosperity of the central and southern states. One reason for this transferal of profits was that the country maintained a low exchange rate for exports. Low exchange rates for exports meant that exporters received an amount of cruzeiros for foreign currency (earned from selling their products) far below the free market rate of exchange. Although the low exchange rates for exports helped keep down inflation in Brazil, as a whole, perhaps it unfairly limited the purchasing power of the country's exporters.

The Northeast has also lost economic benefits to the central and southern states in the marketing of cotton fiber. While cotton grown in the Northeast is made into cloth by the domestic textile industry, the finished cotton products are marketed in the central states of São Paulo, Guanabara, and Minas Gerais, for the most part.

Finally, the Northeast experiences hostile climatic conditions, and is victimized by sporadic droughts which can destroy an entire year's crop. Because the Northeast has a moderately dense population, the droughts usually result in mass starvation among the lower classes, most of whom are unable to migrate out of the area in time to get food.

Because of the devastating effects of the droughts on the lower classes, and to compensate, perhaps, for the drain of profits from the Northeast to the central and southern areas, the Northeast, in the last decade, has been the object of development efforts. The government, with the help of aid from the United States, has undertaken irrigation projects in the region. A government agency, called

SUDENE, coordinates irrigation and other development work in the area. Efforts have been made to build reservoirs for watering the crops during droughts.

Many of those interested in the welfare of the lower class, however, are severely disillusioned with the efforts to improve the economic condition of the Northeast population. Most of the reservoirs which have been constructed do not have irrigation channels to provide the peasants with a supply of water. Most reservoirs are, in fact, constructed so that only the large producers, particularly producers of cotton, benefit from them.

Along with efforts to extend the benfits of irrigation to the lower classes, attempts have been made to help the disadvantaged in the Northeast. One of the major goals of reform-minded politicians in the country, and also of the Alliance for Progress, has been to institute land reform and a redistribution of plots to the laborers. Easy-term loans have also been made, to help small farmers who own land to increase production.

The States of the Interior. The States of the Interior are much less populated than the Northeast, and both Amazônia and Mato Grosso are virtually unchanged by man and civilization. Yet, the resources of these territories are rich and, if tapped, could lead the country away from its dependence on the importation of foreign raw materials. A case in point is the paper industry, located in the central states, which imports wood as raw material, and uses up valuable foreign exchange. If transportation facilities could be developed by extending aid to ambitious entrepreneurs, wood pulp could be obtained in Amazonas.

Transportation problems also plague the frontier area of Mato Grosso. Here, cattle is raised on the open, unpopulated plains, but, in order to process such goods as hides, canned meat, and chemical products, the rancher must use inadequate transportation facilities; these cause damage to the animals in transit and high prices for livestock products.

In sum, we can say that most of the economic problems of the Northeast and the States of the Interior concern the production and profitable marketing of agricultural goods and raw materials. While the population of these particular areas suffers directly from inefficiencies and disparities associated with production and marketing, the country as a whole also suffers, albeit indirectly. It is argued, for example, that land reform in the Northeast would result in greater productivity of small entrepreneurs, since they would own their land and control their products. Greater food production would benefit those urban dwellers throughout the country who now suffer from a shortage of food. If the supply of food were increased, it is further argued, the price of food would drop, and a drop in food prices would significantly reduce one of the main causes of inflation.

The solution of the transportation problem would also benefit the country at large. With better transportation, much of the raw materials purchased abroad for use by industries in the central and southern states could be bought domestically, resulting in greater wealth at home. The foreign exchange, which would be saved by the use of domestic raw materials, could then be used to import vitally needed and greatly demanded manufactured goods which cannot be produced in the country. Again, inflation would probably be relieved by the increased supply of very expensive imported manufactured goods. Similarly, if production of cotton, sugar, and cacao could be made more efficient, the price of these products on the world market would fall, encouraging foreign purchasers to buy them. This would bring more foreign exchange into the country, and facilitate the importation of products needed by Brazilian industrialists.

II. REGIONAL DEVELOPMENT: THE CENTRAL AND SOUTHERN STATES

São Paulo. São Paulo is the wealthiest of all the states, combining the country's most advanced industries and most profitable agricultural crop—coffee. It has a relatively large urban population settled around its industrial complexes; consequently, it has the problem of caring for large numbers of impoverished job-seekers who come to its cities and wind up living in slums. Urban workers in São Paulo are also hurt by the constant rise in food prices of almost 150 percent a year. São Paulo also suffers from a chronic shortage of electricity. The electrical industry is under government supervision but adequate facilities have not been developed.

Coffee exporters in São Paulo are now expressing discontent with the government. Brazil produces nearly half of the coffee sold on the world market but in recent years competition from African exporters has forced prices down. To protect coffee merchants, the government has been buying and stockpiling set quantities of coffee each year. Last year, however, due to the destruction of a large portion of the Brazilian coffee crop, the world price of coffee went up. Now, the Brazilian government is not only profiting from the sale of coffee held in stock, it is also demanding that producers continue to sell their yearly quota to the government at prices which are only partially adjusted to the increase in the world price of coffee.

Minas Gerais. The problems of urban growth in Minas Gerais are comparable to those in São Paulo but are less severe because industrialization and urbanization are less advanced.

The primary industry in the state is mining, and it is seriously hampered by inadequate transportation. Mine owners find it difficult and expensive to get ores to the coast for export. The principal agricultural crop is cotton. Unlike the cotton produced in the Northeast, that produced in Minas Gerais is exported. Efforts are being made to improve production techniques so that Brazilian cotton can compete more effectively on the world market.

Guanabara. The former capital, Rio de Janeiro, is located in this tiny but highly industrialized state. The problems of rapid urbanization are acute in Guanabara. Efforts have been made to ease these problems by improving roads, housing, and schools, but the difficulties remain. Workers and the unemployed are dissatisfied with the lack of progress, and slums continue to grow on the hills overlooking Rio's modern buildings.

Rio Grande do Sul. Rio Grande do Sul has urban areas with problems similar to those already described. Grassy plains comprise large areas of the state, however, so that attention is not centered on the problems of urbanization. The major product of the region is livestock, particularly sheep. The government has recently instituted programs for livestock improvement which may yield important benefits in the future. Like the cattle raisers of the Interior, those of Rio Grande do Sul need better and cheaper transportation to enable them to move their herds from the south to the major processing plants in the center of the country.

Certain aspects of industrialization and urbanization are of common concern to all of the central and southern states, and the extent of government involvement in industry is one of these. Under Vargas and his successors, the government played an active role in fostering domestic investment. At present, the government supplies between 60 and 70 percent of the total investment in the economy each year. The government has also established semi-autonomous agencies and mixed private-public companies in almost every sector of the economy. Indeed, the extent of the government's commitment to industrial development is an important source of the annual budgetary deficit and the continuing inflation. The government not only invests in industry but it also encourages private investment in certain fields through tax incentives. In addition, under the Branco regime, it has taken responsibility for arbitrating labor-management disputes, and administers certain price controls in an effort to control inflation.

At present, industrial growth in Brazil has come to a near standstill. In 1961, the rate of industrial growth was 10.8 percent, whereas in 1963 it was only 0.7 percent. Among the reasons offered for the decline are:

> a decrease in foreign private investment due to distrust of the Goulart regime and to restrictions on foreign entrepreneurs that the regime established;
>
> refusal of the United States and international lending organizations to provide Brazil with the foreign exchange needed for continued development;
>
> domestic problems such as drought and consequent shortages of electrical power, as well as strikes for higher wages.

III. MILITARY EXPENDITURES

Funds made availabe to the military are allocated by the military leaders themselves according to territorial and service needs. Recently, large sums have been devoted to raising military salaries which, under Goulart, had lagged behind increases in the cost of living attributable to inflation.

IV. GOVERNMENT SALARIES

A large civil service is needed to administer the extensive operations of the government. Because of the size of the civil service, civil servants constitute a large proportion of the politically alert population. Recently, government personnel have received substantial salary increases.

V. FOREIGN AID, FOREIGN INVESTMENT, AND REPAYMENT OF FOREIGN DEBT

Public foreign sources of economic support (the International Bank for Reconstruction and Development, the International Monetary Fund, the Inter-American Development Bank, the United States Government) all take anti-inflationary positions. The IBRD, the IDB and the United States Government, for example, are concerned that their support not be dissipated by inflation and economic chaos. They would like to see the government introduce a policy of fiscal austerity that would involve a tightening of credit, introduction of price controls, and improvement of tax collection procedures. Private foreign investors, on the other hand, have seemed to favor government expenditures in the industries in which they are interested, and have been less enthusiastic supporters of austerity.

Since the *coup* and the installation of the Branco regime, government fiscal policies have generally been in line with the former set of views. To the dismay of many domestic entrepreneurs, the government has reduced government spending, instituted price controls, and improved tax collection procedures.

An important factor in Brazil's relations with foreign economic concerns is the repayment of foreign loans. Toward the end of 1963, Brazil began negotiations with its major creditors for loan extensions. These negotiations were successful, with the result that the amount that Brazil must allocate for foreign debt repayment in a given year has been considerably reduced. At the same time, the fact that Brazil was allowed to postpone certain payments increases, in the eyes of foreign creditors, her obligation to meet the new payments on time. Furthermore, Brazil is under some obligation to limit the extent of future borrowing.

VI. DEVELOPMENT PLAN

Successive administrations have undertaken new projects intended to guide the economy toward balanced growth. Sometimes these efforts have taken the form of strengthening a lagging sector, such as the agricultural sector in the Northeast. Efforts have also been made to channel private investment into weak sectors. For example, it was hoped that the moving of the capital to Brasilia would encourage the development of transportation routes in the interior and encourage the exploitation of untapped raw materials.

Nevertheless, faced with the demands of economic elites and politically important groups, the government has found it difficult to achieve the degree of coordination of the various sectors of the economy that is needed for rapid development. The undertaking of a new project almost invariably stimulates controversy on sensitive political and economic issues. Land reform is a case in point. It is easy to get agreement on the need for economic development, but hard to get the agreement of powerful competing groups on a set of concrete steps looking toward this development.

CURRENT POLITICAL ISSUES IN BRAZIL

LAND REFORM

Advocates of land reform argue that too few persons own too much of Brazil's land. They point out that much of the land is not used by the owners, and they argue that this unused land could well be converted by small farmers into plots capable of producing food needed in the domestic market. Extreme advocates of land reform suggest that the land should simply be expropriated and should be paid for by government bonds. Moderate proponents of land reform advocate a heavy tax on unused or undeveloped land that would compel the owners to sell the land or use it.

The land owners, understandably, oppose land reform. They maintain that dividing the land into small plots would cut production. They also suggest that the existing paternalistic relationship gives farm laborers a feeling of security and belonging that they would not have if exposed to the open competition of the market.

INFLATION

Advocates of austerity stress the negative effects of inflation on political stability and economic welfare, and extol the virtues of controls on credit, prices, and wages. Advocates of moderate inflation argue that rising prices encourage investment and speed the adjustment of supply to demand, while the policies associated with austerity would slow or stop economic growth.

By and large, the position of the government has been a moderate one. Government spokesmen have maintained that rapid inflation produces confusion and the misuse of resources, rather than rational investment. Mild inflation, they feel, tempered by price controls, provides stimulation to the market without producing instability or a frenzied investment in sectors that may yield quick profits but certainly contribute little to long-term growth.

FOREIGN AID

The Brazilian government welcomes foreign aid and actively solicits foreign investment. Some Brazilians believe, however, that foreign interests should be more carefully controlled, and that provision should be made for the purchase of foreign concerns at some future date if this seems desirable. They also believe that foreign aid should be accompanied by fewer stipulations regarding Brazil's internal affairs. Opponents of foreign aid and investment argue that acceptance of either necessarily involves a loss of political independence and submission to foreign exploitation.

PRESIDENTIAL POWERS

Leaders in Brazil usually take one of the following positions regarding the power of the President:

The power of the states should be preserved and increased.

Legislative powers should be preserved and increased.

The powers of the President should be increased at the expense of both the states and the legislature.

Whether the powers of the President should be increased or decreased at a given time depends on the policies and programs of the President in question.

Arguments over the powers of the President are articulated in terms of constitutional and legal issues, but behind this debate lie important substantive policy differences. For example, those who believe that centralized economic planning is the road to economic growth tend to favor increased executive power.

WELFARE

Welfare advocates make a case for increased wages, improved social security provisions, improved educational opportunities, aid to small farmers, and other programs that would benefit the less privileged elements in Brazilian society. Opponents of welfare programs argue that resources should be allocated first to the building of an efficient economy and that all Brazilians will ultimately benefit from the growth of the economy.

THE MILITARY IN BRAZILIAN POLITICS

Many Brazilians believe that the military should behave in a way that is neutral and strictly professional. They ask that the military be no more than an efficient tool of the President and the Legislature in times of national emergency. Others believe that Article 176 of the Constitution, which empowers the military to intervene in civilian affairs, makes the military the guardian of the Constitution. There are, however, two different interpretations of Article 176. Moderates feel that the military should step in as a constitutional arbiter only in times of political crisis. The more militant feel that the military are empowered to intervene in the daily flow of political life in order to keep it within the channels prescribed by the Constitution.

5

CHILE

This exercise was designed to be played by individuals who were thoroughly familiar with Chile, with the game to be played, and with their roles in it. Because a number of the players had done research on Chile in connection with a course on national development, we felt that the political system would not need to be abstracted and simplified to the extent that it had been in the case of Brazil. Furthermore, since players would, to some extent, understand the intricacies of the Chilean situation, roles would not need to be defined in a restrictive way. In other words, players could be allowed considerable freedom of action in defining their own roles as they played them.

In the Chilean game, therefore, the goals of individual players were not stated nor were their attitudes on key issues specified. In addition, communication was almost unrestricted; members of the legislative houses were free to institute their own procedural rules; and there was ample opportunity for players to evolve legislation of their own devising, legislation that would, in turn, have an effect on the political and economic system of the simulate. As we discovered, however, it is easy to overestimate the extent of players' familiarity with a game and the country simulated. This exercise proved to be overly complex, given the level of familiarity of the players, and changes in the Rules of the Game had to be introduced during the playing.

One of the values of simulation is that it provides excellent opportunities to demonstrate the application of theory to concrete political situations. For this reason, it is important that the theoretical framework underlying a game be made explicit to the players. Implicit theory can neither be scrutinized nor linked directly to practice. In the construction of the Chilean game, a number of theoretical assumptions were made relating to the political relevance of the overlapping roles of individuals. An individual may play a number of roles relating to various aspects of his life. In the Chilean game, these might include a party role, an economic role, a legislative role, or an interest group role.

The function of such roles is to link the individual with organizations and groups in the political arena. An individual in Chile might have roles linking him with, say, three organizations. Another person might be linked with some of these organizations, and others as well. As we analyzed Chilean society, it appeared to consist of a complex pattern of shared roles and overlapping group memberships. When groups had substantial overlap in membership, and when the roles linking individuals to these organizations were complementary, we assumed that the organizations would find it easy to cooperate with one another. When the roles linking individuals with organizations were conflicting, overlapping membership would be less frequent, and cooperation among the groups harder to attain. In the game, then, we used multiple roles and overlapping memberships to provide the basis on which coalitions of groups would form, weaken, and, finally, disappear, to be replaced by other coalitions. We expected coalitions to break down and yield to new ones when the actors experienced shifts in the priorities they attached to various roles.*

As indicated, the range of roles assigned to players in the Chilean games was quite broad. To start with, all the actors in the game were taken from real life. This marks a change from the Brazilian game in which some of the actors were actual figures on the Brazilian scene and others were prototypical. Brief biographical sketches were provided to inform each player about the background, interests, and behavior of the Chilean actor he was playing. Had more biographical data been available, we would have liked to have had each player do the research on the Chilean actor he was to play.

Interest groups were made to play a significant role in the Chilean game because such groups are important in Chile. Players were assigned appropriate interest-group affiliations, and certain players were designated as leaders of these organizations. The history, present

---

*For a helpful discussion of political roles see David B. Truman, *The Governmental Process* (New York: Alfred A. Knopf, 1951), Chapter II.

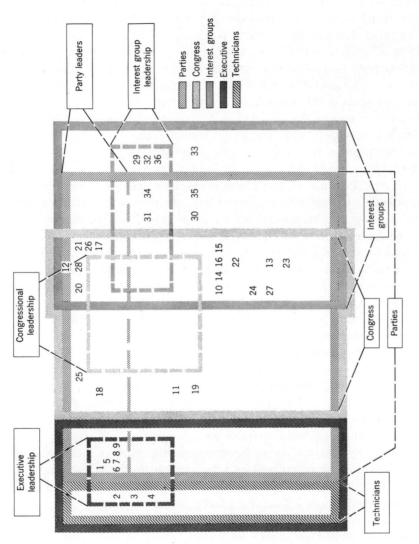

Party leaders

Interest group leadership

Parties
Congress
Interest groups
Executive
Technicians

Interest groups

Congress

Parties

Technicians

Congressional leadership

Executive leadership

Figure 1.

79

policies, and power resources of every prominent interest group were discussed.

Players were also assigned roles in the legislature and in the executive branch. Approximately half of the players had multiple roles which included interest-group, party, and legislative affiliations. The other half had interest-group and party, or party and executive roles. The playing of 2, 3, or 4 different public roles presents a real challenge to player comprehension. To ease the task of grasping the complexity of the Chilean system, we prepared a diagram (Figure 1) indicating the overlapping public roles. This diagram shows the players, at a glance, their position in the political structure. Here each number corresponds to a player (as shown in the Actor Profile Sheet) and the number of roles each player must play is indicated by the overlapping boxes in which his number appears.

Political conflict in the Chilean exercise extends throughout the simulated political system, but it centers in 3 sub-games; a legislative sub-game, an implementation sub-game, and an election sub-game. Speaking first of the legislative sub-game, we chose to introduce a bicameral legislature. One of the simplifications in the Brazilian game was the conversion of Brazil's bicameral legislature into a single-house legislature. To have made the Chilean legislature unicameral, we felt, would have been to distort the political system unduly, particularly in light of the dominance that the Christian Democrats achieved in the 1965 elections. On the whole, the legislative sub-game was successful, although several practical problems arose. The political machinery for coordination between the two chambers was inadequate, and did not develop during the game, despite an evident need for it. The mechanics of coordination might have been eased if the experimenters had thought to provide telephone communication between the two houses.

The implementation sub-game was designed to overcome the problem of getting feedback into the game from the world that is asumed to exist outside the game. For example, it is easy to simulate the decision to build a dam or a power grid. But, since the dam or grid is not actually built, it is difficult to get feedback into the game of the kind that would exist if they were built. Previous exercises had centered around the making of *decisions* (on political and economic policy, on the selection and execution of electoral strategies, on the passage of laws), but no attempt had been made to simulate the events that might follow these decisions.

The implementation sub-game was designed to begin after a bill

ACTOR PROFILE SHEET : 1969

Actor	Party	Leader	Congress	Interest Group	Leader	Executive
1. Eduardo Frei M.	C.D.					President of Chile
2. Alvaro Marfán J.						Technical Advisor
3. Jorge Ahumada C.						Technical Advisor
4. Raúl Sáez S.						CORFO Executive
5. Sergio Molina S.						Minister of Finance
6. Hugo Trivilli F.	C.D.					Minister of Agriculture
7. Eduardo Simián G.	C.D.					Minister of Mining
8. Pedro J. Rodríguez G.	C.D.					Minister of Justice
9. Bernardo Leighton G.	C.D.					Minister of the Interior
10. Gustavo Moncheberg B.	Conser.		Chamber	3 Church		
11. Gustavo Lorca R.	Liber.		Chamber	6		
12. Carlos Morales A.	Radic.	Pres.	Chamber	10 SFF		
13. Manuel Rioseco V.	Radic.		Chamber	10 CUT		
14. José M. Isla H.	C.D.		Chamber	27 CUT		
15. Mario Hamuy B.	C.D.		Chamber	27 SNM		
16. Eugenio Ballesteros	C.D.		Chamber	28 Intell.		
17. Jorge Aravena C.	PADENA	Pres.	Chamber	3 SNA		
18. Mario Garay P.	Social.	Sec. Gen.	Chamber	15		
19. Orlando Millas C.	Commun.		Chamber	18		
20. Francisco Bulnes S.	Conser.	Pres.	Senate	2 SNA		
21. Pedro Ibáñez O.	Liber.	Pres.	Senate	5 SFF		
22. Juan L. Maurás N.	Radic.		Senate	5 SNM		
23. Julio Durán N.	Radic.		Senate	5 SNA		
24. Rafael A. Gumucio V.	C.D.	Pres.	Senate	6 Church		
25. Renán Fuentealba M.	C.D.	Pres.	Senate	7		
26. Baltazar Castro	VNP		Senate	2 CUT		
27. Salvador Allende	Social.	Sec. Gen.	Senate	7 SNM		
28. Luis Corvalán L.	Commun.		Senate	6 Intell.		
29. Victor Braun P.				SNA	Pres.	
30. Enrique Curti C.	Conser.			SNA		
31. Hernán Vídela L.	Liber.			SNM	Pres.	
32. Fernando Smits S.				SFF	Pres.	
33. Eugenio Heiremans D.				SFF		
34. Juan O. Núñez B.	Social.			CUT	Pres.	
35. César Godoy U.	Commun.			CUT		
36. Raúl Silva H.				Church	Cardinal	

had become law. In Chile, the meaning of a law depends, to a great extent, on the way it is administered and enforced. Administrative authorities have a great deal of latitude. How they will choose to administer a law will be influenced by the amount and source of the support for and opposition to that law. After a law is passed, a second round of negotiation is often necessary between executive branch officials and representatives of powerful economic interests.

In the Chilean exercise we assumed that the most important aspect of implementation in Chile is that centering around this second negotiation process. If an understanding is achieved, the political obstacles to execution of the law will have been removed, and only technical obstacles will remain. If an understanding is not achieved, the law might as well not have been passed. Therefore, we chose to let negotiations between government officials and interest-group representatives stand for the entire implementation process. The success of implementation, or the lack of it, would influence the characteristics of Chile in the second phase of the game. The description of Chile in 1969, which the experimenters would give to the players before resumption of the game, would reflect the extent to which legislation passed in 1965 had been implemented.

An additional reason for developing the implementation phase of the game was the stunning success achieved by President Eduardo Frei in the congressional elections. The position of the Christian Democratic Party was so strong that it appeared that President Frei would be able to get legislation through the legislature with little difficulty so long as the Christian Democratic Party did not fragment. Resistance to the President's program, therefore, would tend to express itself *after* the passage of legislation rather than before.

The election sub-game was similar to that in the Brazilian exercise, except that a passive electorate was introduced to supplement the players representing the active elite elements. Five persons associated with the game were not programmed as actors, and took no action in the game other than to cast votes. They were passive recipients of the electioneering in the game, and could not negotiate with the other actors. A passive electorate was introduced because the behavior of Chilean voters cannot be reliably predicted on the basis of the preferences of a small number of leaders and the coalitions formed amongst them. That being the case, a Chilean election (unlike a Brazilian election) could not be simulated realistically, without a broadening of the electorate.

Another innovation in the election sub-game was the players' uncertainty about the number of votes each commanded. We found that in previous exercises, because the number of votes each actor could cast was known, players would sometimes calculate, before the election, which was the winning coalition. In this election, the various political parties knew only what each had polled in the Chilean elections of 1963; they had no way of knowing precisely how many votes each would be able to attract in the forthcoming elections. Just prior to the election, the experimenters determined the final weighting to be given to each party. The determination took the form of an upward or downward correction of the 1963 figures, according to the campaigning skill shown by a party, and the experimenters' assessment of the susceptibility of the electorate to that party's program. Of course, the outcome of the election continued to depend, primarily, on the coalitions formed by the players, and not on the marginal adjustments in votes made by the experimenters.

One of the design questions confronting the authors in this exercise was whether the sub-games should be played consecutively or simultaneously. The question was complicated by the difficulty of combining a legislative session or a public meeting with any other sub-game. Certain kinds of action are easily telescoped in time. For example, in a 2-hour game, a political coalition might emerge which would actually have taken a year to ripen. On this time scale, therefore, an hour equals 6 months. A legislative session can be accelerated in a game, but not to the same extent. An hour of game time might be the equivalent of 3 days, 4 days, or a week of legislative time; but it cannot be made the equivalent, let us say, of an entire session, if such characteristics of the legislative process as extensive debate and prolonged deliberation are to be retained.

We did not fully understand the seriousness of this problem, however, until the game was in its first phase, at which point we became aware of a disjuncture in the pace of events inside the legislature and those outside. To step from the calm of the legislative chamber into the hurly-burly of the Chilean game was to move into another world. The problem stood out more clearly in this game than it had in the Brazilian exercise, because of the more cumbersome functioning of the bicameral legislature. In the legislature, in the Chilean game, bills had to pass not 1 house but 2; and differences between bills emerging from the 2 houses had to be ironed out in conference committees. The problem is not insuperable, but it does need to be recognized and dealt with. A number of remedies are available: avoidance of the bicameral legislature; limitation of the number of bills to be considered;

reduction of the time allowed for debate to a bare minimum; having the legislature meet before the rest of the exercise begins or when other parts of the game are in suspension; or simulating legislative behavior without having the legislature meet. Players have little difficulty moving from one tempo to another; but they cannot be expected to operate at two tempos simultaneously.

Another question related to the ordering of the various sub-games involves the amount of time to be allowed for each sub-game. If several sub-games are played simultaneously, players are likely to feel that they do not have time to give sufficient attention to each sub-game. Yet, these activities are carried on simultaneously by actors in the situation simulated, albeit at a normal tempo, and not in the telescoped time of a game. The experimenters should be braced to discover that however measured they expect the tempo of a game to be, it is likely to pick up speed. New issues will be introduced into the game, and initiatives not anticipated by the experimenters will be taken by some players. These new elements will require a response on the part of other players. The pressure of time upon politicians is often great, but it is rarely as great as in a simulation exercise.

A final consideration influencing the ordering of sub-games is the varying capacities of the different sub-games to draw and hold the attention of the players. Players will be drawn to those sub-games that seem most important, are most familiar to them, that offer them the greatest opportunity for power and prominence, or that are most interestingly developed in the simulate. In the Chilean exercise, the legislative sub-game was familiar and exciting, and players enjoyed it. The processes of implementation, on the other hand, seemed unfamiliar and less exciting. The result was that players were reluctant to shift from the legislative sub-game to the implementation sub-game following the passage of each piece of legislation. They also gave implementation half-hearted attention when they did address themselves to it. The lesson in this is that the legislative and implementation sub-games should not be conducted simultaneously. When a process is strange and new, it should not be forced to compete with other, more familiar, processes for the attention of players. Overnight, during the Chilean game, we made changes that would allow the 3 sub-games to be played consecutively and that would use material from each sub-game as an input for the following sub-game. The Rules of the Game in the following chapter incorporate these changes.

By constructing the final version so that the sub-games were played consecutively, the authors created a situation in which players were required to play their multiple roles in sequence rather than emphasizing each one alternately in response to the needs of the moment. In addition, by running the sub-games consecutively, we made it unavoidable that a player, because of his position in the game, would be busier in one sub-game than in another. An actor representing an interest group, for example, would be centrally in-involved in the implementation sub-game, but only marginally con-cerned with the legislative sub-game.

In summary, then, the sequential arrangement of sub-games sac-rifices some congruence with reality, and runs the risk of leaving play-ers uninvolved, and thus potentially alienated, for part of the game. On the other hand, it allows a player to give a role his full attention while playing it, and reduces the frustration he is likely to experience as a consequence of having to play 2 or 3 roles simultaneously. The experimenters will have to strike the best balance they can, given their purposes; but they must remember that—whatever the arrangement of sub-games—players are not likely to play multiple roles well, until they have had an opportunity to play *each* role by itself and become familiar with it. In the Chilean game, it was only *after* the players had played the party role and *after* they had played the interest-group role that they could cope with the two, simultaneously. The ability of par-ticipants to play multiple roles simultaneously when the situation called for it improved markedly toward the end of the game.

6

CHILE, 1965–1970:
AN EXPERIMENT IN
POLITICAL SIMULATION

[The pamphlet dealing with the Chilean exercise was 91 pages in length, and cannot be reproduced in full. We are including here only the Rules of the Game and samples of other materials such as player biographies, party descriptions, and interest-group descriptions.]

RULES OF THE GAME

PURPOSE OF THE EXERCISE

The exercise is designed primarily as a teaching device to convey information about Chile, to encourage insight into the political processes of a developing nation, and to encourage insight into the general processes of negotiation and political interaction. It is assumed that many of the players will, by the time the exercise is played, have a degree of familiarity with the political situation in Chile, the general problems of Chile's development, the nature of simulation, and the rules of this game.

Players will be assigned roles, and will be obligated to behave in accordance with those roles to the best of their ability.

GAME TIME AND ACTUAL TIME

The game will be played on the following dates: Thursday, April 22, 1:30–5:00; 6:30–9:30 P.M.; Friday, April 23, 1:30–5:30 P.M.

The game begins in the present. It incorporates the results of the recent congressional elections in Chile, and the composition of the legislature in the game approximates that of the present legislature.

Thursday. The playing time on Thursday represents a total of 7 *months.* During the afternoon, from 2:00 to 5:00, the legislature will be in session, representing the Chilean congressional period from May 21 to September 18, 1965. The remaining 3 months in 1965 will be played during the evening. Bills which passed the 1965 legislature will be implemented during this time.

Friday. The game session on April 23 is presumed to take place 4 years later, in 1969. The hours of game time on that date represent 1 year of actual time, and extend through the presidential elections of September 4, 1970. The game will end at 5:30 actual time, which will be November 3, 1970, game time, when the elected administration will take office.

SEQUENCE OF EVENTS

During each of the time periods mentioned above, the exercise will center around a single aspect of the Chilean political process. This aspect will vary from period to period: first, legislation; then, implementation of legislation, and, after that, elections.

Thursday Afternoon:

1:30–2:00	Final briefing and question period before start of game.
2:00–5:00	The legislative chambers meet.

The temporary Presiding Officer will be replaced by a Presiding Officer to be elected in each legislative chamber on the basis of weighted voting.

The administration of President Frei will formally introduce legislation to enact the Frei Plan. (Players have previously received copies of the Plan and the specific bills.

Interest-group members not in the legislature will attempt to influence both executive and legislative branches during the legislative sessions.

5:00–6:30	Dinner break.

Thursday Evening:

6:30–7:00	*Orientation.* Copies of bills passed in the 1965 legislative session, and the forms for the implementation of those bills, will be passed out.

7:00–8:00   Interest groups and the executive meet in their respective headquarters to discuss goals and strategies for implementing the 1965 legislation.

8:00–9:30   *Implementation of 1965 legislation.* The executive will conduct intensive negotiations with the interest groups designated as essential to the implementation of each piece of legislation. During the implementation process, members of the executive branch should be formulating proposals for new bills to be introduced into the 1969 legislative session. These new bills must be ready for distribution to all actors by the beginning of Friday's game session.

Friday Afternoon:

1:30–2:00   *Orientation.* The experimenters will present the players with data indicating what has happened in the 3 years that have intervened since the preceding session. Decisions concerning Chilean developments will be based on legislation passed during Thursday afternoon and the results of negotiations over implementation carried on during Thursday evening. Evaluations of player accomplishments will be made in light of the general nature of the Chilean economy and political system.

2:00   Executive proposals for legislation will be distributed to the actors.

2:00–3:00   *Party meetings.* Actors will now focus on their roles as members of parties competing for electoral success. In light of their satisfaction with actions taken in 1965, and the consequences of those actions, the parties will: (1) Nominate presidential candidates; (2) form alliances with other parties; (3) plan strategies for the 1969 legislative session.

3:00–4:00   *The 1969 legislature meets.* No changes in party strength will be made during this period, and the Presiding Officer will be unchanged.

4:00   Deadline for nominations for President.

4:00–5:00   *Electioneering.* Parties will make campaign appeals to the Chilean masses.

5:00–5:30   *Election.* All meet in Senate chamber to cast ballots.

As soon as the results are announced, the new administration will take office. The new government may wish
to make a statement and to indicate the policy line it
plans to follow in the years ahead.

SPATIAL ARRANGEMENTS

Each party and interest group will be assigned a room to serve as
its headquarters. The President and the executive branch will also be
assigned quarters. Actors may conduct their affairs in the headquarters or elsewhere.

PHYSICAL MOVEMENT

The physical movement of players is unlimited, with the following
exceptions: (a) None but legislators, the President, members of his
administration, and messengers, shall be allowed on the floor of the
legislative chambers. (b) Any group having a headquarters assigned
to it may closet itself in that headquarters and ask other players to
leave.

COMMUNICATIONS

Since movement in the game is relatively free, no messengers will
be used except in the legislative sessions.

The press in Chile is largely a party press. In the game, therefore,
each party is free to bring out issues of its newspaper whenever it
chooses.

Radio Chile (a public address system) will be controlled by the
experimenters. It will be used by them to convey information and
decisions relevant to the game. It may be used by players on request
and at the discretion of the experimenters. The needs of the President of the Republic shall receive high priority attention.

PHYSICAL ACTION

If an actor or group of actors wishes to take physical action
(strikes, demonstrations, etc.), a written request should be conveyed
to the experimenters. The action, if approved, will be announced by
the experimenters over Radio Chile.

CONGRESS AND LEGISLATIVE PROCEDURES

Membership. The legislature of Chile is composed of a Senate
and a Chamber of Deputies. For the purpose of this exercise, there

are 9 members of the Senate and 10 members of the Chamber of Deputies. Players may ascertain whether they are members of the legislature by consulting the Actor Profile Sheet.

Sessions. The temporary Presiding Officer of each House shall call that House to order at 2:15 and proceed with the election of a permanent Presiding Officer. Election shall be by a majority of the weighted votes cast.

Each chamber may recess following a favorable majority vote on a motion for recess.

Each chamber shall adjourn at 5:00.

Each chamber may call itself into special session by a vote of an absolute majority of its members.

Balloting. Balloting in a legislative chamber shall be conducted by the Presiding Officer. The Presiding Officer shall see to it that the results of the balloting are made part of the official record of the chamber. Individual players will have voting strengths in the legislature in proportion to the actual strength of their party or faction in that chamber in Chile. The voting strength of a party will be divided equally among the players of that party. Voting weights of the legislators are assigned on the Actor Profile Sheet.

Quorum. Each Chamber requires a quorum for the conduct of legislative business. In the Senate, a quorum shall consist of ¼ of the members' (12) votes. In the Chamber of Deputies, a quorum shall consist of ⅕ of the members' (29) votes.

Introduction of Bills. Any legislator may introduce a bill in the chamber in which he sits. For this purpose he shall use a proposed legislation form (see following page). A bill may be introduced in either house by a message from the President of the Republic to the Presiding Officer. Bills relating to revenue and expenditures must originate in the Chamber of Deputies.

Debate. Each chamber may establish, by majority vote, its own rules concerning the conduct of its business. Cloture may be moved by any member of either house and is approved by a simple majority of votes cast. If the cloture motion passes, final action must be taken within 3 minutes.

The President of the Republic may declare a bill "urgent," which means that action must be taken on it within 10 minutes of the time that it is introduced.

Passage of Bills. Action is taken on a bill in each house by a majority (weighted) of votes cast. A bill rejected in the chamber of origin (i.e. the chamber in which it was first introduced) cannot be taken up

PROPOSED LEGISLATION FORM

Introduced by _____

Chamber of origin _____ Bill Number _____

Title of bill _____

Text of bill [this space to be expanded as necessary]

1 _____

2 _____

3 _____

4 _____

5 _____

6 _____

Passed in chamber of origin? _____   Vote: (For) _____

Rejected in chamber of origin? _____   (Against) _____

Amendments in chamber of origin _____

_____

_____

Passed in chamber of revision? _____   Vote: (For) _____

Rejected in chamber of revision? _____   (Against) _____

Amendments in chamber of revision _____

_____

_____

_____

Approved by the President

_____

Eduardo Frei

again in the same legislative session. A bill rejected in the chamber of revision may be taken up again in the chamber of origin. If the chamber of origin passes the bill a second time, with a $^2/_3$ majority, it shall be deemed to have passed in both houses unless there is a $^2/_3$ vote *against* it in the chamber of revision. Amendments introduced in the chamber of revision may be approved by the chamber of origin by a simple majority.

The Presiding Officers of the two chambers may establish conference committees at their discretion.

When a bill has been passed by both chambers, it shall be transmitted to the President of the Republic.

Legislative Procedure (miscellaneous). Members of the legislature are free to leave their chambers at any time.

A legislator may raise a point of order at any time if he believes that proper procedure is not being followed, that there are unauthorized persons on the floor, etc. The Presiding Officer shall see to it that appropriate action is taken.

Each chamber has a visitors' gallery. Any player or participant may observe the proceedings from the gallery, but must maintain proper order while so doing. The Presiding Officer may clear the gallery at any time if he feels that the proceedings of the chamber are being impeded.

PRESIDENTIAL APPROVAL OF LEGISLATION

A bill is not law until it has been passed by both chambers and has been approved by the President of the Republic. Presidential approval is signified by his signing of a bill and by his promulgation of it by press or radio.

The President may approve or reject a bill *in toto* or approve or reject portions of it. If vetoed, a bill will be returned to Congress for possible further action.

If the President chooses, he may return the bill to the chamber of origin with his "observations." These observations may, in fact, amount to recommendations that significant changes be made in the legislation.

A bill may be passed over the President's veto by a $^2/_3$ vote in each chamber.

CONSTITUTIONAL REFORM

Constitutional amendments may be passed by an absolute majority in each chamber; when signed by the President, they become official.

In the event that amendments are not approved by the President, they may be passed over his veto by a $2/3$ majority in each house.

POWERS OF THE PRESIDENT

The President has full authority to appoint and dismiss ministers and members of his administration.

It is the responsibility of the President to see to the execution of all laws. He may introduce bills in the legislature through an intermediary, or directly, by sending a message to the Presiding Officer of a chamber.

The President may choose to approve or veto legislation sent to him. (See above.)

The President may not succeed himself in office. (Nevertheless, by virtue of his position in the party, he will be influential in naming the candidate of his party. Most analysts agree that a constitutional amendment enabling the President to succeed himself will not be passed prior to the 1970 elections.)

EXECUTION AND IMPLEMENTATION OF THE LAWS

Implementation of the laws is the responsibility of the President. The enthusiasm and vigor with which he enforces a law is likely to be influenced by the extent of his approval of it. By the same token, the citizens of Chile are obligated to obey the laws of the land; however, unless there is a reasonable degree of support for a law, it may well remain ineffective.

The success of a law, therefore, depends on its implementation, and not alone on its passage by the legislature and signing by the President. Implementation will vary according to the nature of a bill, the degree of support that it has, and the resources that are marshalled for or against it. These factors, the timing of actions taken, and the agreements reached during the implementation process, will serve the *experimenters* as bases for evaluation of the impact of legislation. (Experimenter evaluation of the effect of the legislation and implementation in 1965 may substantially change power relations among actors in 1969.)

In order to implement the bills passed during the 1965 legislative session, the President will appoint a Minister or an Advisor to negotiate with each interest group. A player so appointed will be responsible for recording the results of his negotiations on the "Implementation Sheet" for that interest group.

Each Implementation Sheet will contain:

(a) The name of the interest group to be negotiated with.

(b) The central actors of that interest group.

(c) Key components of the bills passed, on which the interest group in question has had some effect; and broader provisions for the interest group to withhold or submit its total support of the government. [Together these considerations should reflect the total strength of the interest group in relation to the government. Each central actor will signify the degree of his support or opposition to each item by noting his "strong support" with a +2; "weak support," +1; "neutrality," 0; "weak opposition," −1; "strong opposition," −2.]

(d) Space for notation of all formal or informal agreements with the government, including any special provisions for the timing of actions, and any other important comments that would aid the experimenters in their evaluation of the implementation process.

NOMINATIONS, CAMPAIGNS, AND ELECTIONS

Nominations. Any party or coalition of parties may nominate a candidate for the presidency. Nominations, signed by the head of a party, must be in the hands of the experimenters by 8:15 Friday night.

Campaigning. Campaigning will take place during the game on Friday, and may continue until 5:00 P.M. Candidates, or spokesmen for candidates, may apply for time on Radio Chile for campaign purposes. All players will vote, as will the "masses." The masses will be played by a panel of individuals whose voting will be influenced by their estimate of the effectiveness of campaign appeals directed to them. In this exercise, the masses are viewed as passive and cannot bargain with the candidates or their supporters.

Election. The presidential election will take place on Friday at 5:00 P.M. and shall be conducted by the experimenters. At 5:00 all players and the panel representing the masses shall go to the central polling place and cast their ballots. They may remain in the room while the experimenters tally the results on the blackboard. Each *actor* will have a predetermined voting weight in the game which reflects his personal influence and the strength of his party. A player can estimate before the election the weight that will be given his vote by dividing the proportion of the total votes received by his party in the 1963 elections among the players representing the party in the game. However, he will not know the precise weight to be given until the experimenters actually tally the vote.

SAMPLE AGRARIAN REFORM BILL (TEXT)

1. Abandoned land and land that has not been utilized for agrarian pro-
    duction during the past six years shall be expropriated, except lands
    destined to feed church communities. This land may vary in size from
    2 to 50 acres, depending upon the size of the community.
2. Expropriated land shall be paid for over a 25-year period. Payment
    shall be 10 per cent in cash, and the remainder in government bonds.
    The value of the land shall be that figure most recently given to the In-
    ternal Revenue Service by the former owner.
3. Special courts will hear and settle complaints.
4. Nationalized land will be distributed to qualified *campesinos* working
    the land. After a 2-year probationary period, these beneficiaries shall
    receive full title to the land. They shall reimburse the government for
    the value of the land received, such payments to be spread over a 25-
    year period.
5. Unions of agricultural employees shall be formed under the general
    direction of national law.
6. An Association of Agricultural Entrepreneurs shall be established,
    open to all farmers. The Executive Council of the Association will ad-
    vise the government on matters of agricultural policy.
7. Credit facilities and agricultural extension services will be provided for
    small farmers.
8. A system of community farms may be established. In addition to work
    on these farms, the members will be provided with their own houses
    and a plot for growing family food.

SAMPLE IMPLEMENTATION SHEET

A. Interest: SNA

B. Central Actors: Victor Braun, Julio Duran, Francisco Bulnes

C. 1. Degree of cooperation with Earthquake Relief Program.

   2. Degree of cooperation in administering the Amortization Plan.

   3. Degree of informal cooperation in the establishment of:

      a. The Association of Agricultural Entrepreneurs;
      b. Unions of Agricultural Employees.

   4. Extent of re-investment of private profit in the agricultural sector.

   5. Degree of cooperation in reporting personal income tax.

   6. Degree of cooperation with authorities in fixing and paying taxes on
      unutilized private land.

D. Comments and any informal agreements reached between representatives
   of the Government and representatives of the SNA.

INTEREST GROUPS

The director of an interest group may call a meeting of his fellow members at any time.

It is the responsibility of the director to keep an eye on the substance of emerging legislation, and to see that the group makes its preferences known to the legislators.

The position of an interest group on a new law may be communicated to the administration at any time. The Executive Branch will actively solicit interest-group cooperation during the implementation phase of the game.

THE EXPERIMENTERS

The experimenters will be in charge of the game, and will make all necessary decisions pertaining to the game not otherwise provided for.

In addition, they will play certain residual roles in the game to the extent that may be necessary, including:

The military
The comptroller general
The Supreme Court
External actors.

[The material that follows consists of exerpts from the lengthy game packet describing Chile, and is divided into 3 parts. Part I consists of samples of the biographies given to the players. Part II is drawn from the section on interest groups in Chile. The original set of interest-group sketches were prepared by the players as part of the pre-game familiarization process. Part III of the game packet contains a discussion of political parties and a description of current political coalitions.]

PART I: BIOGRAPHICAL SKETCHES OF CHILEAN LEADERS.*

1. *Eduardo FREI Montalva.* President of Chile (1964-1970). Lawyer. Born in 1911. Got his degree from the Catholic University

*From *Diccionario Biográfico de Chile.* Empresa Periodistica de Chile, Duodécima Edición, Santiago de Chile 1962-1964.

at Santiago in 1933. His thesis was "The Chilean Salary System." Was professor of Labor Law at the Catholic University. An ex-member of the Executive Council of the Conservative Party Youth. President of this Council and, later, President of the Falange Nacional. Author of several books including: *Chile Unknown; Politics and Spirit; History of the Chilean Political Parties; The Truth Has Its Time.* Was manager of a publishing company in Tarapacá. Was Minister of Public Works in the GONZÁLEZ Videla Administration. Was elected Senator by the provinces of Atacama and Coquimbo for the 1949-57 legislative period, and reelected by the Santiago Province for the 1957-65 period. Was the Christian Democratic presidential candidate in the 1958 election, and was elected to the Presidency of the Republic in the last presidential election, held September 4, 1964. The Christian Democratic candidate had at this time the "independent support" of the Liberal and Conservative Party.

28. *Luis CORVALAN López.* Senator and Secretary General of the Communist Party. School teacher. Born in 1916. Got his degree of Primary School Teacher from the Chillian School in 1934. He worked in primary schools in Iquique and Valdivia. As a professional journalist, he has worked for the FRAP publications in Santiago, and others in the North. He was Director of *El Siglo* (the Santiago Communist daily) between 1945 and 1948. Since 1957, he has been the Secretary General of the Communist Party. In 1961, he was elected Senator by the provinces of Ñuble, Concepción and Arauco. He has travelled several times through Europe, Asia, and America. An author of several publications of a wide circulation. He is one of the founders of the Journalist Association of Chile and the Chilean Teachers Association.

29. *Víctor BRAUN Page.* President of the SNA. Agricultural Engineer. Born in 1912. He received his degree in Agriculture from the University of New Zealand in 1933. Owner of estates in the Department of Melipilla where he raises sheep. Councilman in Melipilla for 6 years; he was the Alternate Mayor. He has been Director of the Liberal Party since 1936. In 1944 he was elected Deputy for the Fourth District of Santiago. He was on the Board of Directors of the Central Bank. He is President of the SNA (Sociedad Nacional de Agricultura).

PART II: AGRARIAN REFORM AND THE SNA

A. BACKGROUND

Agriculture holds a primary place among Chile's economic problems. As in other Latin American republics, the outmoded patronal system is not conducive to efficient production. In fact, output per worker actually decreased 20 per cent from 1940 to 1953. With an average population increase of 2.5 per cent per year, output is insufficient to meet consumer demand. This drives food prices up. From 1944 to 1954, population increased by 18 per cent while agricultural output increased only 8 per cent. Exports of agricultural products dropped from 14 per cent of total exports in 1951 to 7 per cent in 1963. In 1948, imports of agricultural products were double the value of exports, and the national food import bill has been growing. The low output is due to a number of factors. Ten per cent of the landholders own 86 per cent of the arable land. In a survey, 35 per cent of those holding unused land expressed no wish to increase output. Yet, tax assessments on large landholdings are extremely low, and large holders pay only 14 per cent tax on income. In 1962 and 1963, measures were proposed to tax agricultural land equitably with industry, redistribute unused land (with compensation), and progressively tax personal income of wealthy landholders up to 80 per cent.

Census figures for 1952 showed that the population is roughly 60 per cent urban and 40 per cent rural. The peasantry probably constitutes slightly less than 40 per cent of the population. In rural Chile, there still persists a semi-feudalistic land tenure system that denies to the serf (*inquilino*) any right or way of improving his position. A patron relationship continues between the master and *inquilino*. The system of *latifundismo* (large landholdings) persists; it gives the landowners control not only of the earth but also of the people. It has been customary for landowners to march their peasants off to the polls to vote for the local liberal, radical, or conservative candidate. However, this pattern is changing radically as the broad based political parties seek support for their candidates. This began to be noticeable in the election of Carlos Ibáñez in 1952. In 1957, an electoral reform was approved by Congress to assure the secrecy of the vote and avoid this kind of political coercion. The peasants have been relatively ineffective in organizing unions, or *sindicatos campesinos*, because of the tight control by landowners, but the trend is nevertheless away from this control.

B. GENERAL GOALS

The Frei government maintains that the Agrarian Reform Law, passed during the last years of the Alessandri administration, is nothing more than a mere colonization law. Thus, a real agrarian reform must now be undertaken. The general goals might be stated as follows: (a) An equitable distribution of land; (b) an intensive and rational exploitation to obtain a better and larger agricultural output.

C. PRINCIPLES

The following are the major goals of the Frei Plan:

(1) Agrarian reform is supposed to dignify the farmer.

(2) Land is for those who work it. Those landowners who utilize their land will not be affected by this reform.

(3) Agricultural production is to be increased and improved.

(4) Within a period of 6 years, 100,000 new landowners are to be established. The size of their landholdings will conform to an economic unit of production, the so-called "family property." The new owner will get the land and hold it for a probation period of 2 years; after these 2 years, his land property rights will be confirmed. During this period, the new owner will not have to pay the government for his new property.

(5) Land will be expropriated according to the following criteria: (a) Abandonment of landholdings; (b) partial utilization; (c) social injustice in the treatment of the *campesinos*.

(6) Payment for the expropriated land will be made according to the following system: 10 per cent in cash, and the rest through bonds to be paid during a period of 25 years. The government is now negotiating with the Inter-American Development Bank and other international institutions in order to obtain a guarantee to back these bonds.

(7) The indemnity will be established according to the commercial value of the property declared by its owner; that is, the value he has declared to the Internal Revenue serves as the basis for the amount of taxes he pays.

(8) Special courts will hear complaints in matters of expropriations for agrarian reform. These complaints can be made only on 2 issues: (a) The validity of the expropriation, and (b) the amount of the indemnization fixed by the government. These courts are composed of one judge of the local Court of Appeal, an agricultural engineer appointed by the Ministry of Agriculture, and a representative of an agricultural society.

D. THE SNA POSITION

The SNA has published statements which oppose the agrarian reform project. In a public declaration, the following points were made:[1]

(1) Difficult times and problems provide fertile ground for the inventors of panaceas. Solutions are proposed passionately and unthinkingly. (2) Property is "the base through which the society is sustained," rather than an anti-social privilege. Passionate prejudices against the rural owners agitate the class struggle between the farmers and the workers. (3) Agrarian Reform involves a transgression against the rights of property that is bad for both owners and nation.

Addressing a regional agricultural association, Victor Braun, President of the SNA, declared that "we (the agricultural entrepreneurs) must be united in order to make our experience felt in the discussion of the legislation, as well as in the elaboration and implementation of the plans. . . . The government of Mr. Frei should accept this collaboration and constructive criticism for the benefit of Chilean development."[2]

PART III: POLITICAL PARTIES AND COALITIONS

THREE CATEGORIES

(1) The rightist groups (Conservatives and Liberals).

(2) The Centrist-Radicals (whose leaders are becoming more conservative); Christian Democrats (who are leaning to the left in their democratic reformist approach).

(3) The leftist groups like FRAP (Frente de Acción Popular). Of the parties in FRAP, the Socialists and Communists are the most important; others are the PADENA (Partido Democrático Nacional), a nationalist, non-Marxist group; and the VNP (Vanguardia Nacional del Pueblo), a small "charismatic" type of organization, led by Baltazar Castro. Its slight support comes mainly from the province of O'Higgins.

Since 1955, the Christian Democrats have rocketed into prominence. The dominant parties of the previous decade, except for the

[1] See *El Mercurio*: Santiago de Chile, January 24, 1965, p. 39.
[2] *Ibid.*, Santiago de Chile, March 13, 1965, p. 33.

Communists and the Socialists, have shown a marked decline. The strength of the Christian Democrats is balanced somewhat, however, by the fact that the other political parties, while differing radically on goals, have all joined the opposition.

Generally speaking, the patterns of internal party organization are similar. Parties are national, rather than regional, organizations. The regional assemblies designate members to national congresses, which decide the general outlines the parties will follow. Usually, these congresses designate the President and the members of the Executive Council that are to lead the organization.

In addition to their centralized organization, most parties maintain communication with members through the use of partisan newspapers.

CHRISTIAN DEMOCRATIC PARTY

The philosophical origins of the Christian Democratic Party are to be found in the social encyclical *Rerum Novarum* of Leo XIII, and in the encyclical *Quadragesimo Anno*. This philosophy acknowledges the importance of achieving minimum living standards and working conditions for the working classes. These views of the Catholic Church, together with the influence of the Spanish Revolution and the works of the French philosopher Jacques Maritain, created a ferment among the younger generation of the Conservative Party. They formed a progressive "Conservative Youth Movement" and, in 1938, officially split from the Conservative Party, becoming the *Falange Nacional*. The new party, with its democratic social and political ideals and its traditional religion, attracted progressive intellectuals, trade unionists, and modern industrialists. Subsequently changing its name to the Christian Democratic Party, it came to occupy a left-of-center position in the Chilean political party spectrum.

The Christian Democrats are fundamentally a Christian party, but stress their "non-confessional" nature, thereby drawing upon a cross section of all groups along the social spectrum. Their religious and democratic idealism is displayed in a social concern for all classes. Seeing the defects in the communistic and capitalistic systems, the Christian Democrats advocate a "middle way" or "third alternative." It consists of the involvement of the worker in management and ownership, the promotion of intermediate groupings between the individual and the state, and state intervention to restrict the power of large economic interests. The state exists in a mixed system to plan, to orient, to lead. Internationally the Christian Democrats support Latin American political and economic integration and a just partnership with the United States in an independent and equal sense. In summary, the Christian Democratic Party believes in a social and religious pluralism, in an open society, and in the necessity of cooperation domestically and internationally.

The rise of the Christian Democratic Party in Chilean politics has been spectacular, owing, perhaps, to its excellent internal organization and to the increasing dissatisfaction of the middle classes. Its support is drawn essentially from middle groups, intellectuals, and some of the industrial and rural lower class. The party obtained 15.9 per cent of the popular vote in 1957; 19 per cent in 1958; 15.9 per cent in 1961; 22.8 per cent in 1963; and over 53 per cent in 1964, when it had the support of the Conservatives, the Liberals, and some of the Radicals. It obtained a surprising first majority in the last congressional election: 42.3 per cent of the total vote. Women and young people have constituted an essential factor in the party's electoral success. The party has promised sweeping social reforms within the existing framework. Like the parties mentioned above, it supports the principles of the Alliance for Progress.

The party controls *La Nación*, the semi-official government newspaper.

THE FRAP COALITION

Socialists and Communists. These parties have declared themselves in strong opposition to Frei. "The government of Frei is not even reformist; it is reactionary,"[1] declared Mario Garay, Undersecretary General of the Socialist Party. They contend that behind the constitutional reform lies the totalitarian mind of the Christian Democrats. *The Popular Promotion* announces the creation of new bureaucratic institutions to "feed the hungry stomachs"[2] of the Christian Democrat bureaucrats for doing tasks that ought to be performed by the municipalities. The Socialists and Communists favor the nationalization of mining, industry, and banks, as opposed to the Chileanization program proposed by the Frei government which they term a facade to cover the same interests that have always governed Chile.

The declarations and demonstrations against the Christian Democrats that have been made by the Socialist leaders are stronger

[1]See *Ercilla* 1952, Santiago de Chile, December 9, 1964, p. 18.
[2]*Ibid.*

than those made by the Communists. However, in whatever form their opposition takes place, it can be predicted that it will be "within the rules of the game," and that it will not be completely blind; that is, these parties will favor in Congress those measures proposed by the Christian Democrats with which they completely agree. These may include the so-called Patrimonial Tax (a major tax reform project), the diplomatic and commercial relations with the Soviet bloc, some of the social development proposals, etc. But, for the most part, these parties feel that the Christian Democratic reforms are too mild, not going to the core of the problems.

Both parties maintain a strict internal discipline (this is especially true for the Communists), and can be expected to continue in the FRAP coalition, despite their long standing differences. However, the Castroite line accepted by some leaders of these parties can be expected to gain more adherents. The resignation of Senator Jaime Barros from the Communist Party on the grounds that it is ineffective and following bourgeois trends is a reflection of this development.

After 3 consecutive defeats of Salvador Allende (1952, 1958, 1964), the FRAP does not appear to have, at this point, a real "leader" on whom to rely for propaganda purposes. The fact that they have maintained their congressional representation in the 1965 election is a real achievement for the Socialists and Communists, as many observers have commented.

7

DURHAM, NORTH CAROLINA: THE SIMULATION OF AN URBAN POLITICAL SYSTEM

Simulation has enjoyed wide application in the social sciences, and yet its potential is still not fully appreciated. The approach we have experimented with is not confined to national systems, but can be used in connection with any political system. In an effort to demonstrate its versatility, the authors decided to simulate an urban political system.

A number of attempts have been made to simulate the processes of an urban community.* The Durham exercise differs from these in a number of ways, but perhaps most prominently in its attempt to simulate the processes of an actual rather than a hypothetical community, and in its introduction of players playing the roles of actual community leaders.

An advantage of this approach is that the community being simulated serves as a check on the experimenters and prevents them from designing a completely unrealistic simulate. As the design takes shape, the designers can check their model again and again by observing the actual community. Furthermore, simulation of a real community rather than an imaginary one spares the experimenters

---

*For example the "Metropolis" game developed by Richard L. Meier and colleagues at the University of Michigan, and the "Woodbury" game developed by Bradford Seasholes at the Massachusetts Institute of Technology and Tufts.

the need to invent vast quantities of data. If a question comes up about land-use patterns, tax rates, or voting behavior, an answer can usually be found by an examination of data on the community. Those who use these data can also be confident that the characteristics of the community depicted by actual data are internally consistent. The more extensive and complex are the data manufactured for a hypothetical community, the greater is the likelihood that internal inconsistency will creep in.

This approach has the further advantage that, as in the case of the simulation of a national system, the investigator is more or less forced to center his attention on the dynamics of the situation simulated. He will find himself asking a different range of questions than researchers placing less emphasis on the dynamics of political systems; and he will focus on actors, their resources, actions taken, group interaction, patterns of communication, and so on. A system cannot be miniaturized unless its dynamics are understood. This means that categorization and static analysis have little to offer.

The city chosen for the experiment was Durham, North Carolina. Durham was selected because its proximity to the University of North Carolina in Chapel Hill would ease the problems of data gathering and analysis, and because a good deal of material on Durham was already available at the University.

The collection of data on Durham and the analysis of the political system of that city were undertaken as a class project in a course on community politics. Since researchers sometimes have trouble seeing things they are not looking for, it was suggested at the outset that students be alert to the following in conducting their research:

Statistical data
Historical data
Norms and attitudes in the community
Inputs from the environment into Durham, and outputs from
    Durham into the environment
Social structure
Political structure
Financial and economic structure
The functioning of elements in the Negro community
Important actors in Durham
Important formal organizations
Role of informal organizations
The communication system in Durham

Patterns of influence in the community
Patterns of conflict and cooperation

A great many hours were spent in Durham going through records and interviewing people, and a great many more were spent in trying to organize the data and impressions gathered. These first phases of the project—fact-finding, description, analysis—were valuable in themselves and amounted to a careful field study of Durham. It is no small undertaking to try to understand and to describe the political system of an entire city. Linking the simulation project to a university course proved to have many advantages. Students studied the literature on urban politics and found that it helped them understand Durham. In turn, the study of Durham provided a needed corrective for assigned reading. The students who conducted the research (primarily graduate students in political science and city planning) gained a working familiarity with Durham and, hence, were better able to understand not only the analysis going into the game, but also how to play the game itself. The research served as the means by which players were socialized into the game.

The actual design of the game was the product of a smaller planning group. If the pressure of time had been less, greater use of collective effort might have been made during the design stage. A good deal of the thinking that went into the construction of the Durham game is set forth in the game description in the following chapter.

DURHAM, 1965-1969

The Durham game was played on April 29, 1965. There were 44 players in the game, and close to half of them were members of the class that had been studying Durham. Individuals who had become most familiar with Durham were given the more important roles, for the most part, and they helped to keep the game in tune with the behavior of the actual actors in Durham.

Politics in Durham is the story of the relationship among key groups. The Durham game, therefore, was organized according to those groupings rather than on a geographic basis, such as wards or precincts. The game was played in 2 parts, the first in 1965 and the second in 1969, game time. The election of 1965 and a scheduled annexation referendum took place within the context of the politics of consensus that has characterized Durham for a number of years. Between 1965 and 1969, however, the game design posited an increase of political tension in Durham, particularly within the Negro community, and the emergence of a serious challenge to the continued dominance of the Establishment.

In the simulations described earlier, the active participants were leaders, and the exercises might be described as "top leadership" games. In the Durham simulate, secondary leadership was incorporated. Leaders had to compete for the support of sub-leaders since the sub-leaders were assumed to have access to different groups of voters. Decisions by sub-leaders and by members of the passive electorate would determine the outcome among competing leaders and their respective programs.

The game itself was exceedingly involved as it unfolded, and took a great many turns that had not been expected by the experimenters. All that can be done here is to suggest its general drift. As the game began in 1965, the Negro and white leaders of the Establishment looked forward confidently to the election and the annexation referendum to follow it. The Negro leadership was not worried about Smith*, a young Negro businessman running for a seat on the City Council in opposition to them. Smith had the support of the Negro student organizations and gained the endorsement of the Central Labor Council. The Council agreed to support him if he would take a stand in opposition to annexation. Smith agreed. Despite Smith's efforts, the SNRC, the major political organization in the Negro community, refused to endorse him.

There were contests for 4 City Council seats (First Ward, Third Ward, Fifth Ward, and at large). Two of the races were not notable. In the First Ward, however, the segregationist candidate lost badly, and in the Third Ward, Smith was defeated, even though he received 39 per cent of the votes. The results showed that the Establishment was still in control of the situation, but Smith's showing suggested that there were votes to be had in an appeal to Negro militancy.

The annexation issue received a good deal of attention before the election, and became the primary focus of the game after the election. The Mayor devoted time and energy to explaining the merits of annexation, and members of the white Establishment gave annexation their full support. The members of the Negro Establishment were also favorably disposed, and *The Durham Press* backed it. Opponents of the measure felt that they were fighting a losing battle.

Smith proved to be the most effective opponent of annexation. He

*The names of all individuals have been changed.

tied the issue to his demand for the paving of streets in Negro sections and the improvement of sanitation facilities. With telling effect, he argued that "the Negroes of the Third Ward will pay for the services of the new annexed areas." The City Manager and the City Planner prepared data designed to counter this argument, and the Mayor announced that, if annexation carried, he hoped to spend the revenue from the annexed areas in Negro districts. Discussion revolved around the question of the economic implications of annexation, with proponents arguing that it would be a source of income, and opponents arguing that it would be a financial burden on the city.

Despite the favorable attitude of the members of the Negro Establishment toward annexation, the political effects of Smith's arguments could not be ignored and, in the end, the SNRC came out in opposition to annexation. This made the difference, and the annexation referendum was defeated.

As the 1969 phase of the game began, most of the players sensed certain changes in the political complexion of the community, and realized that votes now tended to lie more to the political left. The white Establishment, feeling the need to project a more favorable image, formed a new organization, the Committee for a Progressive Durham. To avoid the development of a schism, a deliberate effort was made to court Negro support.

The SNRC engaged in soul searching, also. Members argued that the organization was losing its hold on the Negro community, and was in danger of becoming ineffective as a guiding mechanism. The only way out, they insisted, lay in the development of a broader base of Negro support associated with the adoption of a more militant ideology.

A public meeting was called, at which the urban renewal issue became linked with public housing. The debate swirled about such questions as, where the public housing was to be located (in a predominantly Negro area or in a white area); who would or would not profit by the purchase of the land by the city; to whom would the housing be open (whites, Negroes, or both); whether or not it would be low-cost housing; were there alternatives to public housing; were the wealthy Durham Negroes more concerned with their pocketbooks or the needs of their race; and so on. Though these issues were discussed, they were not necessarily clarified. As the election approached, it became harder to know what the issues were, and where individual candidates stood on them. The confusion of the individual voter when confronted by a multiplicity of complex, technical, issues was nicely simulated. As members of an electorate are sometimes wont to do when confused, they voted against the incumbents. The Mayor and incumbent City Council members were ousted.

The white Establishment showed a good deal of vitality, and managed to fight off the challenge successfully. A member of the white Establishment, for example, was elected Mayor. Nevertheless, it was a harder, closer, and more bitter contest than in 1965. An observer could suspect that the era of easy Establishment control of the affairs of Durham might be drawing to a close. An alliance emerged between liberal whites, liberal Negroes, and labor, but did not harden into a firm and reliable coalition. Organizational machinery for the coordination of the liberal Negro and liberal white elements did not take shape, and the alliance began to come apart at the seams.

The potential voting strength of this alliance was never wielded effectively, and one of the explanations for it lay in the absorption of key players with the power struggle in the Negro community. Over the years, the SNRC had been the primary instrument through which the members of the Negro Establishment had exercised their leadership. The challenge was now direct and clear. The emergence of a new militancy in the Negro community outside the SNRC began to be reflected within the SNRC. It could not isolate itself from these new currents, and the key question became: Which way would the SNRC go? It was torn between the growing militancy of its clientele (over which it was trying to exert leadership), on the one hand, and its long-standing ties (including financial support) with the prestigious, wealthy business-oriented Negro leadership, on the other. Individual members of the Negro Establishment who belonged to SNRC appeared to be faced with the choice between voting for their race at the expense of their economic interests, and voting for their economic interests at the risk of alienating themselves from the broader Negro community. The unity of the SNRC was shattered and, in the end, it chose not to endorse any candidates.

The exercise vividly portrayed the breakdown of community consensus. If the white Establishment finally emerged victorious, it was an expensive victory. No longer could its members count on an easy control of ⅓ of Durham's population through the SNRC. If it is correct to say that the Negro community holds the key to the politics of Durham, then a political upheaval in that community could not fail to have far-reaching implications for the city as a whole. The pattern of tranquility and the habit of settling issues in the community by agreement among a handful of elite elements were both shattered. The old leadership was no longer able to govern easily and effectively, and the new leadership was not yet strong enough to replace it.

The confusion of rank-and-file voters was related to the confusion of the leadership. One of the functions normally performed by community leaders is the development of a "party line" that will interpret events for the rank and file, and guide their thinking and voting. When conflict within a community is clear cut, there are likely to be competing "party lines," each seeking adherents and offering alternative interpretations of current events and issues. In this exercise, on the other hand, no such "party lines," however specious, emerged, and an analysis of votes cast, coalitions, and statements by voters, gives evidence of the confusion attendant on a situation of political transition.

ANALYSIS

The Durham exercise can be analyzed from many points of view. As noted earlier, the use of simulation does not commit the observer to a particular conception of *the* proper technique for analyzing the events of a game. For example, the exercise might be analyzed in terms of negotiation and bargaining. How was a strong bargaining position communicated and recognized? Who initiated the discussion leading to the conclusion of a bargain? Why were some deals soft and others firm? What were the negotiating and bargaining techniques that were used? It might also be studied in terms of coalition formation or electoral strategy. What were the bases on which coalitions were formed? What types of electoral strategies are identifiable in the game? For example, inter-elite in-fighting was so extensive and active that campaigning before the passive electorate was virtually overlooked by some of the candidates. Members of the passive electorate, in turn, voted heavily for those candidates who had troubled to present their case and show them some attention. Is this a recognizable pattern? How did the candidates endeavor to persuade voters that theirs was an ascendent star and that an opponent had little chance of success in the election? How effective were the two organizations that emerged during the campaign: "The Duke Faculty for a Better Durham," and the "Committee for a Progressive Durham?"

What was the thinking that led to the establishment of these groups?

Another way in which the Durham exercise could be analyzed would be in terms of the resources available to the different actors and the way in which these resources were used.* Certain resources were peculiar to the individual playing a particular role. If the individual understood his role well and could begin effectively playing it as soon as the game began, this was an advantage to him. The city planners, for example, were specialists who were able to begin functioning even while others were still developing a feeling for their roles. Several players had developed a high degree of familiarity with Durham politics during the research stage of the gaming cycle, and the possession of this special knowledge and information was a significant resource. Confidence and familiarity with simulation allowed others to get off to a fast start. Personality was a factor of importance throughout the game, but there were, nevertheless, limits to its effectiveness. Several persuasive and determined players found themselves in back eddies of the game and never succeeded in getting to the center of things.

A number of non-personal factors influenced the prominence of players in the game. "Saliency," or visibility, was important. The player whose role was special or unusual in some way (the Mayor, for example) was able to establish himself quickly in the minds of others. Players whose friends, allies, and interests were set forth in the scenario, were able to get off to a faster start than those who had to elaborate their own goals and probe for sources of support.

The number of votes a player could command was an obvious resource, and central to most of the bargaining in the exercise. It was not always easy to trade one's votes for concrete game advantages, however.

Hard-working and efficient friends proved to be a valuable resource for players. The pace of the game was fast, and anything that saved the time of a prominent actor was a resource. Players who were able to press others into their service and who had lieutenants to whom they could delegate responsibility were fortunate. The Mayor was disadvantaged by the absence of skilled political lieutenants. The members of his staff were highly competent on specialized technical matters but were not interested in serving as political aides.

The telescoping of actual time into shortened units of game times

*See Robert Dahl, *Who Governs?* (New Haven: Yale University Press, 1961).

worked a greater hardship on some players than on others. The players on the Mayor's staff, for instance, mostly graduate students in city planning, had clearly defined roles as "experts," and were able to start functioning as soon as the game began.

Before long, however, tension began to arise between the political leaders and the experts. The former wanted quick answers on technical problems, and the latter, holding to standards of workmanship, insisted that careful and reasonable answers could not be produced on such short notice. In other words, technical processes were not telescoped as easily as were political processes. With foresight, however, this problem could probably be overcome in the game design.

It was an important resource for a player, if the appeals that he could make were such as to strike a responsive chord in other players. The ideological climate of the game necessarily helped some players and hampered others. The White Citizens Council was ineffective; was perhaps doomed to be so. The support that it would have been able to call forth in Durham was not adequately simulated in the game. As a result, the segregationists tended to be isolated, and there was hesitation over making alliances with them even for limited tactical purposes. In contrast, Brezezinski, a labor leader in the 1969 phase of the game, succeeded in offering slogans and symbols that some players responded to. Indeed, there may even have been a greater response in the game than would have been appropriate for Durham in 1969. Players were somewhat casual in aligning themselves with Brezezinski and did not appear to assess the costs of such action carefully. Perhaps this was because the game lacked a "future." There would be no tomorrow, when players would have to pay for mistakes they made today.

As a resource, wealth played a less compelling role in the simulate than it normally plays in Durham. It is difficult to get rewards and penalties properly distributed in a simulate, yet if their allocation is not approximately correct a distortion is introduced into the exercise. How does one build significant wealth differentials into a game and make them psychologically convincing to the players? Perhaps, if a monetary system had been built into the game, this difficulty would have been overcome. The decision to omit such a system, however, was based on the belief that the players might become so absorbed in the economics of the game that its political aspects would get short shrift.

Status, a resource in most communities, was imperfectly simulated in the Durham exercise. Status that is *achieved* during the game normally provides no problems. The difficulty comes with status that is *ascribed* to certain players because their counterparts in the full-scale political system do, in fact, have status. For example, members of the white Establishment had to compete for support within the community that would normally have been given to them without question. Other players were unimpressed by the fact that Establishment players were said to own banks, insurance companies, and real estate. They did not pay them the deference that their counterparts in Durham enjoy. The problem could have been dealt with at the mechanical level, of course; by specifying that a given bloc of votes must always be allocated to the Establishment. Nevertheless, it would be more satisfying to deal with the problem by improving the quality of the role playing. A more extended familiarization period might have obviated the difficulty.

Tradition is a "resource" for those actors and interests in a community whom tradition supports. The incorporation of tradition into a simulate, however, creates problems for the designers. What substitute mechanisms can be found that would have an effect in a simulate identical with that which tradition has in the system simulated? Tradition places obstacles in the way of any but incremental changes, and ensures that some things will continue to be done because they have been done in the past. In Durham, for example, tradition helps account for the solicitous approach of community leaders to certain established interests. Tobacco is a pillar of the Durham economy and tobacco interests are well cared for. Interestingly, however, those persons familiar with the Durham power structure who were interviewed during the design of the game reported that the tobacco interests were scarcely ever heard from. The tobacco companies, then, are not an active factor in the political life of Durham; yet, their interests are adequately cared for. How does this happen? The explanation seems to be that everyone knows that the tobacco companies are important to Durham and that anything that hurts those companies might hurt Durham, as well. It has become traditional to take care of the interests of the tobacco companies and, therefore, explicit communication is rarely necessary. "Influence" exists and concessions are made in the virtual absence of demands and "pressure" in the usual sense. We sought to cope with the situation by failing to include the tobacco companies as an active interest, while specifying that City Council members and others would be fully aware of the importance of tobacco to Durham. We tried to incorporate "tradition" by making it a part of the value system of certain actors.

Information was an important resource in this game. Those who possessed information about Durham and what was happening in the game were able to use it as an instrument to gain ascendency. Those who were not "in the know" could be little more than pawns in the hands of the knowledgeable. The term "information," as used above, includes anything deemed to be fact, regardless of its accuracy. Information and misinformation served almost equally well as instruments of influence, since the ability of players to distinguish between the two was low. The level of misinformation in the game seemed surprisingly high, considering that the number of players was restricted and the exercise took place on a single floor in a building. The explanation probably lies in the fact that the tempo of the game offset (perhaps more than offset) the reduction in the number of actors and the physical scope of the game. With time foreshortened and decisions having to be made quickly, fact had a hard time catching up with fiction.

The process by which information was diffused among the players was highly imperfect, and, for that reason, extremely interesting. On several occasions, information relevant to a decision had been available in the game for as long as 30 minutes without being brought to bear on the making of the decision. There is no automatic process to ensure that information will flow to the point where it is most needed. Indeed, it may be everywhere in a game but where it is needed. Also noteworthy was how much of the information and opinion relevant to decision making was confined to face-to-fact communication and never appeared in the newspaper and was never heard on the radio.

Questionnaires were administered to the players at the end of the 1965 phase of the game, and again at the end of the 1969 phase. In the excitement at the end of the game, and with the announcement of election results, players did not respond to the questionnaires carefully, so that the 1969 results had to be disregarded. The Durham data for 1965, however, provide some interesting results.

The questionnaire asked a player to rank himself on the following:

(1) The extent to which he was an active and vocal participant in the game.

(2) The degree of his personal involvement in the exercise.

(3) The extent to which he was a leader in game activity.

(4) Whether he would have preferred another role.

(5) Whether he had enjoyed participating in the exercise.

(6) The extent to which he had visited other rooms during the exercise.

During the game the staff of observers made independent rankings of players on some of the same variables (frequency of visits, leadership, apparent involvement, etc.) in order to have a check on the subjective impressions of the players.

Two clear clusters of correlated variables emerged. First, the responses to questions 1, 3, and 6 had a high degree of association with one another (see Table 1). Players who felt that they had been leaders in the game also felt that they had been vocal, had been active, and had interacted a good deal with other players. A player who ranked himself low on one scale would be likely to rank himself low on the other two, as well. Second, involvement (question 2) and player enjoyment (question 5) were closely associated but these responses were not significantly associated with the measures of leadership (see Table 1). This suggests that the leadership and activity a player ex-

TABLE 1
Durham, 1965: $N = 30$*

	(1)†	(2)	(3)	(4)	(5)	(6)
(1) active-vocal	1.000					
(2) involvement	+.316	1.000				
(3) leadership	+.827	+.388	1.000			
(4) role assignment	−.199	−.180	−.159	1.000		
(5) enjoyment	−.005	+.451	+.126	−.083	1.000	
(6) number of visits	+.591	+.104	+.562	−.051	+.016	1.000

*An N of 30 includes members of the passive electorate. When the same patterns were studied, omitting the members of the passive electorate, the cluster relationships were weaker but were still evident. With an N of 30, an r of .449 or greater is significant at the .01 level. An r of .349 is significant at the .05 level.

†Numbers correspond with sequence in extreme left column.

hibits in a game (1, 3, 6) depend heavily on the role to which he has been assigned; whereas a player's sense of involvement and enjoyment (2, 5) may depend primarily upon the personal characteristics of the player, and not upon the role to which he has been assigned. If this conclusion is correct, then it has important implications for simulation involving human players. It would mean that players can become involved in a game and enjoy the experience, and, presumably, benefit from it, without needing to play a role of importance. This finding is in keeping with our casual observations. Not all the players want to be "chiefs;" many are content to be just "Indians." The individuals who are alienated in the course of a game are not those who play minor roles, but those who feel they have been left out of the game altogether. In the Brazilian game, as noted earlier, it was the foreign actors who felt isolated and frustrated, not the unimportant actors.

Role playing was better in this game than in previous ones. There were culture barriers to cross, but at least there were no national boundaries. In addition, because many of the players had been studying Durham for the better part of a semester, there was a higher degree of player socialization than ever before. Nevertheless, roles were still imperfectly played. Players who were not supposed to be important became important during the game. They achieved status and significance; others enjoying ascribed status and significance failed to live up to their billing. The game had a certain drift to the left that may have been associated both with weak role playing and with the liberal "set" of the academic community in which the exercise was conducted. On the other hand, it may have had to do with the design of the game, the inherent dynamics of the situation simulated, or simply that there was more sound, fury, and excitement to be had on the left than on the right.

The Durham exercise, unlike some urban simulations, involves players in multiple roles. This is far more characteristic of urban politics than is a design allocating one role per player. An individual in the Durham game might be a Negro and play a role in the Negro community. He might also be a banker and a member of the City Council. Another player might be a white businessman, be associated with anti-labor activities, and be a member of a segregationist organization. In this type of game, players may, under some circumstances, add roles while playing, or may shift priorities among established roles.

This would be appropriate if the actor being modeled were not himself fully committed to a set of role priorities.

The type of simulation represented by the Durham exercise has important implications for certain kinds of research, but its most immediate and striking application is in the field of training and education. To operate effectively in a complex social, political, and economic environment, the individual must understand the working of that environment. This is true whether we are speaking of a public health officer, a police chief, a city manager, a city planner, or an interested citizen. An individual who does not understand the political dimensions of his environment is likely to be ineffective and will probably not understand *why* he is ineffective. If an individual is to function in a community with reasonable assurance of success, it is not enough for him to be well trained in his special area of competence; he must also understand the structure and the political processes of the community.

The versatility of community simulation and the ease with which it can be adapted to various purposes help explain why its training potential is so great. Annexation was made an important issue in Durham. An urban redevelopment issue was built into the 1969 phase of the game because it appeared that such an issue would probably confront Durham by 1969. If we had so desired, however, either of these issues could have been replaced by a fluoridation issue, a school bond issue, a zoning issue, or virtually any other kind of issue.

Just as issues can be added and subtracted once the basic game is developed, so, too, a variety of sub-games could be added or subtracted. The sub-game devoted to the Negro community is highly developed in the Durham exercise. Had the experimenters chosen, it could have been elaborated further or could have been simplified. It could remain the only important sub-game in the exercise or it could be supplemented by sub-games dealing, let us say, with the tobacco companies, Duke University, or business conflict. The experimenters, in short, can plug into the main game or leave out whatever issues or sub-games they choose, depending on their purposes. They can make a simulate deal with almost anything they choose, and that is the secret of the versatility of simulation.

In time, perhaps, there will be an array of community simulation exercises that schools of public administration, public health, or planning can draw upon for various purposes. A trainee who is to be sent to a particular kind of community would be involved in simulations involving that type of community. An official, going to a large city, might be involved in the simulation of the political system of that city; New York, Philadelphia, Boston, Los Angeles, for example.

As part of the familiarization process, students could do research on individual actors or sub-games and update the simulate from year to year.

8

DURHAM, NORTH CAROLINA, 1965–1969

The simulation exercise contained herein was prepared for teaching purposes and was conducted by the Political Science Department of the University of North Carolina on April 29, 1965.

An effort has been made to simulate the political structures and processes of Durham. In this game, Durham has been treated as a slack political system in which potential political resources have often not been exploited; an exception is the Negro sub-community in which political resources have been carefully employed. In this community, the degree of political organization is much greater than is typical in southern cities.

The game is intended to incorporate typical roles into the simulation exercise, and to allow the players considerable freedom to devise new strategies and make new allies during the course of the game.

The game is played during 1965 and 1969 in order to allow an interim period during which changing trends in the physical and demographic character of Durham set the stage for changes in political behavior in the city.

All actors in the game are fictitious. Any resemblance to actual persons is merely a coincidence, and simply reflects an effort to cast players in "typical" roles.

ACTORS

Actors will be of three kinds: Leaders, sub-leaders, and the electorate. Leaders and sub-leaders will interact freely among themselves and will make appeals to the electorate. The electorate will be composed of passive players whose only function will be to observe the happenings in the political arena and react through balloting at election time.

LEADERS

There are 35 active players in the 1965 game and 40 in the 1969 game. In addition, there are 4 passive players in both games. The chief impact of the active players on the game will be made through taking action, consistent with their role descriptions to achieve their objectives. Each actor will have specific resources (though not expressed in quantitative terms), and will be able to engage in strategy with other leaders that is intended to maximize his ends. Several actors will have more than one role, giving them considerable choice as to the ends toward which to devote their resources at any given time. The activity the leader may engage in is indicated later under "Leader Activity." Obviously, some of these types of activity are characteristic of some kinds of actors and not of others.

Leaders may communicate freely among themselves; leaders will be assigned to rooms with other leaders on the basis of the degree of interaction found in Durham. Rooms will be provided for: Negro leaders, white economic leaders, city hall, segregationists, and labor.

THE PASSIVE ELECTORATE

In the first part of the game, the passive electorate will consist of 7 actors representing the passive white vote. There will be no passive Negro vote. The passive white electorate will be broken up into 3 categories: Labor, white collar, business and professional. The 7 actors, with their respective voting strengths, will be distributed as follows:

Interest Group	Actor	Votes
Labor	Permanent passive	9
White collar	Brezezinski	2
	Sloan	3
White collar	Permanent passive A	15
	Permanent passive B	6
	Zimmerman	1
Business-professional	Permanent passive	20

Voting strength of an individual is determined on the basis of the numerical and voting importance in Durham of the segment of the population he represents.

In the second game, actors Brezezinski and Sloan become active participants with voting strengths of 5 each. The permanent passive labor actors' voting strength is reduced to 7. Actor Zimmerman becomes an active participant with voting strength of 1; permanent passive actor A's voting strength is reduced to 14; permanent passive actor B's strength remains the same. The permanent passive business-professional actor's voting strength remains constant, giving the following passive electorate for 1969:

Interest Group	Actor	Votes
Labor	Permanent passive	7
White collar	Permanent passive A	14
	Permanent passive B	6
Business-professional	Permanent passive	20

Each passive actor will have a different combination of characteristics representing a substantial body of the voting public. The passive electorate will normally remain in one room, taking no initiative whatever. However, if a leader wishes to make an oral presentation to only a part of the passive electorate, he will be assigned another room in which to do so, after which, that portion of the passive electorate will return to the original room. The passive electorate will not provide any feedback prior to elections, with the possible exception that the mass media may send a reporter to talk with the electorate and report trends which may be observed. Actors will recognize that reports of the media may be biased. Members of the passive electorate may *not* make any deals with anyone as to vote trading or anything else.

The passive electorate will select a chairman (solely for mechanical purposes of the game) who will control the access which candidates and sponsors of referenda campaigns will have to the electorate. Such candidates may appear before the electorate at any time on a first-come-first-served basis. However, if other campaigners are waiting to be heard, each individual will be limited to a 3-minute presentation. After each presentation, each member of the passive electorate

RULES OF THE GAME

(Exercise to be played April 29, 1965)

Time Span and Sequence of Events
    The game begins May 2, 1965, the day after the primary election.

2:00–3:00	Election campaign
2:15	Simulated Negro Relations Committee (SNRC) meets to endorse candidates. The results of the meeting may be announced at any time prior to the election.
3:00	Election of City Council.
3:10–5:00	Annexation campaign (preliminaries for this may actually begin earlier).
5:00	Election on Annexation issue
5:15–6:30	Dinner break
6:30	Players reconvene. The time will be January 1, *1969*. A sheet will be distributed describing the events which have taken place during the intervening 4-year period. Players will resume the game at 7:00 on the basis of this information.
7:00	Game resumes
7:00–10:00	Activity leading to municipal election of May, 1969. Discussion and negotiation on pressing economic and social issues.
8:30	Deadline for filing by candidates for the election.
9:00	Primary, if one is needed.
9:45	Election
9:55	Announcement of election results.
10:00	End of exercise.

LIST OF ACTORS, IDENTIFICATION, AND VOTING WEIGHTS

Actor	Roles	Votes 1965	1969
1. Adams	President, SNRC; President of Bank	3	3
2. Bailey	Member, SNRC; President, Savings and Loan; City Council	2	2
3. Carson	Executive Secretary, SNRC; college professor	2	2
4. Davis	Chairman, Education Committee, SNRC; college employee	2	2
5. Harriss	National leader of civil rights organization; Negro	2	2
6. Jones	Negro labor leader; lost challenge to SNRC candidate in 1963	2	2
7. Smith	President, Business College; opposing Bailey in 1965	2	2
8. Franklin	Leader of Negro college students	3	3
9. Fox	Negro; Vice Chairman, Neighborhood Council #1	5	5
10. Bird	Negro; Chairman, Neighborhood Council #2	4	5
11. Doe	Economic conservative; at-large candidate in 1965	1	1
12. Mayer	Mayor; tax accountant	1	1
13. Mann	Downtown Merchants Association leader	1	1
14. Worthington	Chamber of Commerce leader; speaks for tobacco, textiles	1	1
15. Lander	Board of Realtors' spokesman	1	1
16. Arrow	Former councilman; President, Committee on Civil Rights; Chairman, pro-annexation organization	1	1

Actor	Roles	Votes 1965	Votes 1969
17. Wright, Sr.	Ideological leader of pro-growth white Establishment; insurance company official	1	
Wright, Jr.	Son of Wright, Sr., more liberal; takes role 1969		1
18. Mrs. Perry	Attorney; property interests; on Council	1	1
19. Mrs. Rogers	Old family; wealth; commitment to community welfare, especially education; university trustee	1	1
20. Nelson	Savings and Loan audit; Council 1965	1	1
21. Caldwell	City Manager	1	1
22. Rivers	City Planner	1	1
23. Smart	University official (1965 only)	1	
Bright	University faculty member (1969 only)		1
24. Workman	Secretary of Central Labor Union, visible spokesman for national labor view	1	1
25. Campbell	Operates sandwich shop; pro-labor; Council, 1965	1	1
26. Chase	Owns construction company; City Council 1965	1	1
27. Rice	University sociologist; precinct politician; running for Council 1965	1	1
28. Murphy	Liberal Realtor; Council 1965	1	1
29. Wilson	Writer; articulate spokesman for opposition to annexation; lives in suburbs	0	0
30. Murdock	Chairman, White Citizens' Council, Tobacco company foreman; running for Council against Chase 1965	1	1

LIST OF ACTORS, IDENTIFICATION, AND VOTING WEIGHTS
(*Cont'd*)

Actor	Roles	Votes 1965	1969
	The following players are passive in 1965 and will sit with the passive electorate; they will become active leaders in 1969		
31. Zimmerman	President of university conservative students organization	2	5
32. Brezezinski	Labor organizer, employed by new industry in 1969; brings new active image of labor role in politics; liberal ideas	2	5
33. Sloan	White Citizens Council, segregationist	3	5
	The following players are passive throughout		
34. Passive labor		9	4
35. Passive white-collar vote		15	14
36. Passive white-collar vote		6	6
37. Business-professional vote		20	20
	The following players join the game in 1969		
38. Baldwin	Negro, spokesman for white collar people; upwardly mobile	0	41
39. Tanner	Negro leader; a shop steward	0	4
40. Biggs	Unemployed Negro	0	1
41. Wesley	President, University student body, liberal	0	2
42. Green	University clerical staff; divergent ideology from faculty or students	0	1
43. Editor	Represents mass media	0	0
44. Reporter	Assistant to editor	0	0

may if he wishes, ask 1 question of the speaker. The chairman of the electorate will keep time on the speakers, and usher in the succeeding campaigners in the order they are lined up outside. Printed handouts may be circulated to the passive electorate on an unlimited basis.

The operation of the passive electorate simulates mass meetings and mass media appeals to unorganized voters. A presentation to part of the electorate would simulate campaigning among neighborhood groups. Feedback to the press simulates the kind of "pulse taking" which actually occurs during a campaign.

ELECTIONS

The first election occurs on May 15. When the game begins, candidates have already filed, and the primary election has been held. The 7 members of the City Council and their opponents in the May 15 election are:

Wards	Incumbents	Opponents
First	Chase	Murdock
Third	Bailey	Smith
Fifth	Murphy	Rice
At-large	Carlton	Doe
At-large	Campbell	Doe
At-large	Mrs. Perry	Doe
Mayor	Mayer	unopposed

The "ward" candidates run against each other, while all of the 4 at-large candidates run against each other for the 3 places.

The votes of all players are weighted. The number of votes each player may cast *may* change between 1965 and 1969. Therefore, the number of votes to be cast in elections during these 2 years is indicated on the List of Actors. The weights for the passive electorate have been given above.

Each player is obligated to cast only the number of votes authorized. When the ballots are distributed, each player will vote the number of votes he has at his disposal by writing in the number of these which he intends to vote for each candidate. Players may split their votes among the candidates, as they see fit, and it is assumed that passive electorates A and B will not vote for the same candidates.

They may confer with each other in order to trade voting information. Players will sign their ballots with their game names as a check on the balloting. The experimenters will serve as election judges, and ballots will be cast at a designated point near the Experimenter Center. They may be transmitted in person or by messenger. Voting weights will be the same in the annexation election as in the May Council election.

Candidates who wish to run for the 1969 election may file at any time between 7:00 and 8:30 P.M. for any of the 7 Council posts (including Mayor) by delivering to the experimenters a slip of paper indicating for which post they desire to run (First, Third, or Fifth Ward, at-large, or Mayor), accompanied by the filing fee of $7.80. This paper must be signed by the candidate. Campaigning may begin as soon as the candidate has filed.

In the council election of 1965 *only* the SNRC-endorsed candidates will receive a bonus of 10 votes, since changes in the political structure after 1965 will lead to reduced bloc voting. Actors numbering 1-5 constitute the SNRC.

The rationale for the weighting of votes is as follows: The Negro community in Durham tends to vote as a bloc for candidates endorsed by its leadership (represented by SNRC). There is no appreciable organization of voting blocs within the white community.

Adams, as president of the SNRC, is given 3 votes in both games.

Bailey, Carson, Davis, and *Harriss* are members of the SNRC and are accorded 2 votes in both games.

Jones and *Smith* are also given 2 votes, for although they are not SNRC members, they are recognized leaders in the Negro community with appreciable influence.

Franklin, as leader and spokesman for Negro college students, is given 3 votes in both games, since the students are active in securing increased Negro political participation.

In the 1965 election, the SNRC-endorsed slate of candidates is awarded 10 extra votes, representing the high degree of influence this organization has. This influence is expected to decline as other leadership emerges within the Negro community. The decline is represented in the 1969 game by providing *Baldwin* with 4 votes, *Tanner* with 4 votes, and *Wesley* with 2 votes, removing the 10-vote bonus from direct SNRC control.

Fox and *Bird* are sub-leaders within the Negro community. *Bird* is arbitrarily given 1 less vote in the 1965 election. He is given an additional vote in 1969 to reflect population increase.

Doe, Mayer, Mann, Worthington, Lander, Arrow, Wright, Sr., Nelson, Perry, Rogers, City Manager, City Planner, Smart, Workman, Murphey, Wilson, Murdock, Campbell, and *Chase* are given 1 vote in each game as leaders of the less organized white community. *Wright, Jr.,* and *Bright* replace *Wright, Sr.,* and *Smart,* respectively, in the 1969 game, each having 1 vote.

Biggs is introduced into the second game to represent the potential emergence of militant Negroes. Since this development is open to question, he is given only 1 vote.

Green is introduced in the second game to represent a third ideology, one possibly present on the University campus, and different from that of the faculty and/or students. He is given only 1 vote.

Because of the high organization of the Negro community's political participation, all their votes are distributed among active participants representing the Negro community in both games.

The passive white electorate is broken into 3 categories: Labor, white collar, and business-professional. *Zimmerman, Brezezinski,* and *Sloan* play part of the passive white electorate in the 1965 game. In 1965, *Brezezinski* and *Sloan* are part of the passive labor group, with 2 and 3 votes respectively. The remaining 9 votes are cast by a third individual. In 1969, because of the expected increase in activity on the part of both professional labor organizers and the segregationist labor element, *Brezezinski* and *Sloan* become active players with 5 votes each, and the passive vote of labor is reduced to 7 votes.

In 1965, the passive white-collar vote is divided among 3 individuals—A has 15 votes, B has 6 votes, and *Zimmerman* has 1. The 15–6 division is designed to provide less opportunity for bloc voting. *A and B are not expected to vote for the same man. Zimmerman* represents the conservative student element at the University which is considered passive in 1965, but active in 1969, because of its expected increase in strength and organization. He is given 1 vote in both games. The votes cast by A and B in 1969 remain the same as in 1965.

The business-professional passive electorate is represented by 1 individual with 20 votes in each game.

The breakdown of 14 votes for labor, 20 votes for business-professional, and 22 votes for white collar in the 1965 game represents the relative strengths of the white passive voters of Durham. The passive vote for labor is reduced to 7 in 1969 because it is expected that labor will become more active. This activity is represented by giving Brezezinski 5 votes, and Sloan 5 votes—for a total labor vote of 17. White-collar and business-professional passive strength is expected to remain the same.

LEADER ACTIVITY

The following actions may be taken by leaders, following the procedures specified in each case. If an action being contemplated does not clearly fall within this list, the leader may apply, in writing, to the experimenters for permission to take the action.

1. *Make Statement to the Media.* The statement should be as brief and to the point as possible, in order to avoid excessive strain on reproduction facilities. The statement should be written. The media will print or announce such statements at the discretion of the editors. Editorial material must be so designated by the editor. The editor will publish newspapers and will also have available a radio channel known as Radio Durham.

2. *Make Agreement with Other Leaders.* A leader may enter into substantive agreements with other leaders (within the limits of his roles). He may either (a) honor or not honor the agreement later; or (b) announce the agreement, keep it secret, or deny its existence. A written copy of all substantive agreements shall be submitted to the experimenters.

3. *Solicit Information from City Hall.* Any leader may ask for information from the offices of the City Planner, the City Manager, and the urban renewal officer. Such information, in very brief form, will be provided and will be regarded as official and accurate. City hall will *not* provide conflicting information intentionally. It may, however, deliver interpretive information with factual information. That is, when the phraseology is: "In the judgment of the city planner ..." etc., this will be taken as official city policy, but not necessarily fact. If the information is: "There are 1,500 Negroes in the 'X' annexation area," this will be regarded by all actors as fact. Short of withholding information, city officials may use their discretion as to the degree of enthusiasm with which they will cooperate with various leaders.

4. *Circulate Written Documents.* Leaders may produce and distribute written information at any time.

5. *Speech to Electorate.* This is an actual oral presentation, as indicated above, limited to 3 minutes if necessary, and followed by the answering of any questions from the electorate. Answers must be

brief and germane. This will simulate statements at public meetings, appearances on radio and television (See foregoing section: The Passive Electorate).

6. *Request to City Manager.* Oral or written requests may be made to the City Manager for those kinds of action which are within the normal discretion of managers. The Manager may take whatever action he deems appropriate, such as (a) doing nothing, (b) referring the matter to the Council by discussing it with individual councilmen or with the entire Council in an informal conference, (c) taking the action requested, or (d) taking some action related to, but other than the one requested. If he does *either of the last two things,* he *must* post the action on the City Manager's bulletin board and notify the press of action taken.

7. *Propose Action in the City Council.* The City Council, composed of the Mayor and 6 councilmen, will never hold a formal meeting, though it may confer with the City Manager as to actions he may take. Council action will be simulated through the following 2-step process: (a) Action may be formally presented to the Council (in the form of the resolution or ordinance desired) over the signature of any 15 leaders (signatures may *not* be forged); and *two copies must be signed.* (b) The proposal will then be circulated among *all* 7 councilmen, each of whom will sign his name, followed by either a "yes" or a "no" vote. If there are 4 or more "yes" votes, the measure will be deemed passed, and the sponsor of the measure will post one copy on the City Manager's bulletin board and deliver the other to the press. If the measure fails, a copy will be given to the press.

The above procedure simulates actual decision-making procedure, in that much of the city's business originates outside the Council. When conveyed to the Council for formal decision, the normal procedure is for the Council to reach a consensus prior to the formal meeting of ratification. Formal decisions are normally taken unanimously, and debate and parliamentary maneuver have no part in the "legislative" process. Thus, actual Council meetings, as in most cities, are *pro forma* only. The game will simulate the real decision process rather than its formal aspect.

8. *Petition to the Durham County Legislative Delegation.* Any leader may present any petition to the legislative delegation in two copies, signed by himself and, if possible, others. This petition will be delivered to an experimenter. The experimenters will determine

whether and when the measure is introduced into the legislature, and enacted. The more signatures on the petition, the better the chance of getting the matter introduced into the legislature. If the measure is enacted, the experimenters will post 1 copy on the City Manager's bulletin board and give the other copy to the press.

9. *File Suit.* A suit may be filed in the appropriate court by giving two copies to the experimenters, setting forth the issue and the legal grounds on which action is desired. If and when the court issues a decree pro or con, a copy will be posted on the City Manager's bulletin board and another given to the press.

10. *Pressure in Washington.* Action may be sought from the appropriate Washington agency of the United States government by presenting the request to the experimenters in writing, in two copies. If Washington takes any action on the matter, this will be noted and attached to the original request and returned to the petitioner. The petitioner may then release information as to the response from Washington when and how he sees fit, but the release must be substantially accurate. If he wishes to post a copy on the City Manager's bulletin board, he must first obtain the permission of the City Manager.

11. *Private Physical Action.* Leaders who have resources under their control as set forth in role descriptions may utilize these resources in any way they see fit, subject to the approval of the experimenters. This approval may be given orally in response to an oral request. The leader will then be able to announce his action to the press, to the electorate (orally), or simply pass the information by word of mouth. This covers such events as moving out the tobacco factories, constructing a new plant, etc.

12. *Physical Actions in Categories Not Included Above.* Such actions may be taken only with oral or written approval of the experimenters. In such cases, the instructions of the experimenters as to the procedure to be followed must be observed.

CITY MANAGER'S BULLETIN BOARD

The City Manager's bulletin board simulates the City Hall Reporter, and is a safeguard for publishing of key events. The bulletin board may be used only in accordance with the rules indicated above. However, the City Manager may initiate action which is not petitioned for, and in this event, he will announce this action on the bulletin board, while also making the announcement to the press.

EXPERIMENTERS

The experimenters may inject new elements into the game at their discretion. If they do so, all players will be informed through available media.

REPORTING

A staff of observers will circulate throughout the game and will be given access to all rooms, conferences, and proceedings. The observers will not participate in the game in any way, and information given to them will be treated as confidential.

ANNOUNCEMENTS ON PUBLIC ADDRESS SYSTEM

When the editor wishes to broadcast over his radio channel, the announcement will be preceded by: "This is Radio Durham." When the experimenters wish to communicate with players, they will first say: "This is the experimenters." In the latter case, the information may be regarded as factual.

POLITICAL ISSUES AND POLITICAL DYNAMICS

DURHAM, 1965

Durham, 1965, is dominated by two main features of the political situation. First, there is a very high degree of elite agreement. This agreement has several bases. Members of the Establishment, white and Negro, are business oriented. This orientation more or less guarantees that they will tend to see most questions in a common light. For example, they want new industry because it is good for business.

The second major feature of Durham politics, related to the first, is that rank-and-file voters are not organized. There has, to date, been no effective challenge to the established white-Negro financial oligarchy. The mass of voters remain unorganized because there has been no active competition among them by different groups seeking their support.

The Negro community, numbering ⅓ of the Durham population, appears to be quiescent in its acceptance of the leadership of the Negro financial group through the Committee on Negro Relations. This organization, in serving Negro needs by organizing them for electoral purposes, holds the balance of power, and, thus, is the key to Durham politics. On the other hand, there is a dissident leader challenging the Negro established leadership in the 1965 elections. Also on the scene is a national Negro leader who resides in Durham and finds himself in an ambiguous position. He receives a great deal of his financial support from the Negro financial elite; this aids his national position, and he is understandably loath to jeopardize that support by engaging in activities in Durham potentially unfavorable to the Committee on Negro Relations.

"Durham, 1965" will revolve around two issues: An economic issue, and the up-coming elections.

ECONOMIC FACTORS

The growth of Durham is an economic issue which affects important groups in Durham differentially. Urban redevelopment is a growth issue which is supported by the politically dominant groups in Durham. However, most of the decisions on urban renewal have been made during the recent past, and so, presently, this does not seem to be an area of conflict. Relocation may be a potential area of conflict if Negro relocation begins to threaten residents of white neighborhoods, or if a shortage of relocation housing develops.

At the present time, controversy over growth is focusing on the annexation of areas immediately adjacent to Durham. A local author, resident of the section over which greatest controversy has arisen, is spokesman for those who live in areas to be annexed. He opposes annexation primarily because he wants to avoid city tax rates. He also feels that in areas such as his, which is a middle-class residential area, the resident owners of undeveloped real estate will be forced to sell their property because of inability to pay frontage rates for water, sewage, and curb and gutter installation. He feels that outsiders, such as Durham realtors, have the capital to purchase these forced sales and to pay for the city improvements. They will then develop this property, making profits which should rightly go to the resident owners.

Many taxpayers of the city of Durham are also opposed to annexation. Since annexation requires a city bond issue to pay for the extension of city services to these areas, tax-conscious Durham residents are opposed. Under North Carolina law, only city residents can vote on the annexation proposal. Therefore, it is for support of these taxpayers that the opposition campaign is being waged.

Other groups in Durham, such as the White Citizens Council, as well as economic conservatives, see big government at any level as a potential economic threat. They are, therefore, ideologically opposed to any proposal which tends to increase the scope of government. This includes annexation.

Generally, the opponents of annexation are scattered about. They are unorganized at present and do not work through "established" organizations. They do not have the resources of wealth or prestige. They may have the resource of votes, however, since most of their communication seems to be of a grass-roots, word-of-mouth character.

The pro-annexation people are those who would benefit from growth. A bigger Durham means more retail and wholesale sales, a larger labor pool, a larger tax base, and higher real estate values. The merchants' association, the Chamber of Commerce and Industrialists, the Negro financial interests, property-holding old Durham families, the Board of Realtors, the newspapers, and the Mayor and city administrators all support annexation. These elements make up the Durham Establishment, and their representatives on the City Council are the dominant force in Durham politics. They have the resources of wealth, prestige, time, and energy on their side; however, since the final decision rests with a city-wide election, votes are the crucial factors to be influenced by these other resources. The pro-growth group also has effective access to the information channels and formal news media. The Citizens Committee for the Annexation Bond Issue is the *ad hoc* organization coordinating the Establishment's campaign among the voters.

Other groups are in favor of annexation for ideological reasons. Included here are Duke progressives, white liberals, and middle-class, good-government forces. Increasing the size and tax base of the city would mean a more efficient use of resources and increased governmental services over the long run.

Two major groups in Durham could go either way on annexation. Dissident Negro leaders may see the annexation of areas in which whites are in the majority as a threat to the electoral balance of power of the Negro community. The established Negro leadership at present seems to favor annexation. However, if increased pressure is brought to bear on this issue by dissident Negroes, the Committee on Negro Relations may have to take a stand against annexation (or refuse to make any commitment on the issue), in order to head off the challenge to its leadership. The Committee opposed the recent unification bond issue.

The Central Labor Council could also go either way on annexation. The leadership of the CLC is of the liberal-labor variety. In recent years they have lost the support of rank-and-file labor as segregationists won control of the tobacco workers' locals. These conservatives are against annexation. Other members of the rank and file are against annexation because of the tax issue. The CLC has indicated that it hasn't yet decided on annexation; it has hinted that it is waiting to see if the city will reverse its stand against across-the-board pay increases for city employees before it decides.

Thus, lack of consensus within labor and the Negro community enables the leadership of these 2 groups to bargain with those who are pro and con on annexation. The rewards offered by either side have to be sufficient to motivate the CLC and the Committee on Negro Relations to attempt to withstand dissident elements by getting off the fence. It may prove to be most practical for both sets of leaders to abstain.

Durham actors line up on annexation as follows:

Pro-annexation	Anti-annexation	Undecided
White economic elite	Articulate residents of areas to be annexed	Central Labor Council
Negro financial elite	White Citizens Council	Negro community
City Council	Conservatives	
Newspapers	Restless taxpayers	
Citizens Committee for Annexation Bond	Dissident Negroes	
Mayor and Administration		
University progressives and liberals		

The annexation issue will be decided in a city-wide bond referendum. This will take place in a special election on June 15, 1965.

THE ELECTION OF 1965

On May 15, 1965, there will be a local election to elect the Mayor and 6 members to the City Council. Votes are counted for all candidates on an at-large basis. However, the City Council seats are divided between 3 at-large and 3 so-called ward seats. The only difference between these is that candidates for the at-large seats can live anywhere in the city, and they all run against each other with the 3 top vote-getters being elected. Only 2 candidates oppose each other for each ward seat and they have to live in the ward that they run for.

The incumbent Mayor and most of the incumbent councilmen are without serious opposition. The only serious challenge is for the Third Ward seat.

The Third Ward is completely within the Negro district, and a Negro has held this seat continuously since 1953. The present incumbent, who has held the seat since 1957, is a member of the executive committee of the Committee on Negro Relations and president of a savings bank. He is being challenged for this seat by a Negro who is president of a local business school. The latter is focusing his campaign upon the inadequacy of city services in the Negro areas and upon opening higher-status city jobs to Negroes. He notes that the most ancient city firefighting equipment serves the Negro areas and that the two highest-ranking Negro policemen still pound beats.

This challenge may be a major threat to the established leadership. Both challenger and incumbent will appeal to the students and the Negro Neighborhood Councils for their support. The students are generally somewhat more militant than the Negro leadership, but they have been allied with the Committee on Negro Relations in the past. Their support is needed to provide volunteer manpower in conducting campaigns in the Negro areas. High Negro turnout rates are necessary for Negroes to outweigh the unorganized but numerous white voters. Negro Neighborhood Councils have not been politically active in the past, but they are concerned with the quality of services provided by the city in Negro neighborhoods.

The nationally known civil rights leader who resides in Durham is, like the college students, more militant than the Committee on Negro Relations leadership. Because of his position in the national organization, he is somewhat tied economically to the Negro financial elite, and has been drawn into the local Committee on Negro Relations as a sub-committee chairman. The insurgent candidate in the election puts him in a position in which he has to decide whether to support increased militancy or not.

In the Third Ward contest, the incumbent, because of his ties to the Committee on Negro Relations, very clearly has the edge on the resources of money, status, and organization. The Committee in the past has proved itself a very effective voting league. Its support of candidates, made public a day before the election, has been enough to swing the Negro vote. However, the record of wins has been upset in elections where two Negroes were competing for the same office. So, even though the incumbent has the edge now, the challenge represents a long-term threat, by dramatizing the Committee's lack of militancy.

In the white community, the absence of serious opponents to the incumbents indicates the low degree of political conflict in Durham, and is a consequence of a non-partisan election system. Similarly, the fact that this challenge candidate has not organized a broad-based group to compete with the Committee on Negro Relations in the Negro community illustrates this lack of conflict. In general, the elements of conflict found in the economic issue and in the election are more logically classified as latent community conflicts which have not as yet become widespread enough to disrupt the Establishment's management of community affairs. Increased economic and social change may make these elements of conflict manifest by 1969.

INTERVENING TRENDS, 1965–1969

NEGRO COMMUNITY

After the election of 1965 and the strong challenge made by a dissident, it is projected that the more "militant" in the Negro community will continue to make demands on both our Simulated Negro Relations Committee (SNRC) leadership and the community as a whole. Within SNRC, the erstwhile challenger and his supporters attend all meetings and speak out on every issue. In some cases, he has forced the leadership to admit that more action has to be taken. For example, as a result of increased pressures, the SNRC leadership demanded that the city provide transportation for Negro students attending previously all-white schools. After 18 months of negotiation with the City Board of Education and the City Council, transportation facilities were provided. As a result of this kind of action, a dissident, actor Smith, was appointed to the political committee of the SNRC.

As a whole, the Negro community, by 1969, has changed its character somewhat. There is a growing Negro middle class filling in the previously wide gap between the leaders and the working class.

This group, while not matching the white middle class in income and education, has taken on middle-class values with its white-collar positions and increased education. With these, come middle-class demands. They have also become more politically aware and less willing to have their decisions made at the top and communicated to them in a "this-is-your-best-interest" manner. The Neighborhood Councils, formed in 1965, have continued to grow and have become active on a variety of issues. They have sent representatives to City Council, Planning Board, and Board of Education meetings. This in itself has been seen by observers as a threat to SNRC's leadership and as a fractionalization within the Negro community. White leadership, in general, has found that while it is still mandatory to consult with the SNRC, often this is not sufficient. Other members of the Negro community must be consulted.

In addition to the Neighborhood Councils, the Negro students have become more vocal. The summer of 1965 saw large-scale demonstrations in North Carolina led by the Rev. Martin Luther King, Jr. Students from the Negro college were heavily represented in these rallies and marches. Harriss, the nationally known figure, was the leader of the students in all these cases. Since 1965, his national organization has become less militant. (Some students say it has "gone the way of the Urban League.") The student organizations in town have, however, retained their militancy. They have on occasion spoken of their dissatisfaction with the SNRC positions; they have also sent representatives to various city meetings. Harriss has been walking the thin line between the SNRC and the students.

As the 1969 Council election approaches, Bailey, the incumbent on the Council from the Third Ward, has chosen not to run. Carson, Professor of Science at the Negro college, and official of SNRC (an unsuccessful candidate for County Commissioner in 1962 and 1966), announced his candidacy. Smith, the opponent of Bailey in 1962, has also announced his candidacy; and the Negro community is talking of selecting someone to run for a Council seat at large. The decision has to be made concerning who this will be.

ECONOMIC DEVELOPMENTS

The tobacco industry in Durham, as in the rest of North Carolina, has declined somewhat in the past 4 years. In addition to unemployment due to this decline, the tobacco industry has become more automated, and automation has led to increased unemployment.

Attempts to recruit industry were made. Two of the main attractions in the area are the Research Triangle Park and the Environmental Health Center. Because of the nature of these two establishments, Durham was more attractive to light industry and industries with research interests. The movement of Southeastern Electric to Durham in 1967 relieved some of this unemployment but not all. There were plenty of jobs for white-collar workers but not nearly enough for unskilled labor. Durham's unemployment had risen from 10 per cent in 1965 to 13 per cent in 1969. North Carolina's "Right to Work" Law was still in effect. This, plus the unemployment situation, made it necessary for the union affiliated with the electronics industry to see that the Durham plant was organized. During the past year (1968), the union, AEIOU (American Electronics International Organization of Unions) had sent an organizer to Durham; he had soon become involved in local politics, attempting both to increase the strength of the Central Labor Council and establish his union's influence base. The union representative has been an articulate spokesman on education, labor, and housing industries.

Chief among the issues in Durham in 1969 is urban redevelopment. Three sites have been chosen for discussion before the Planning Board and the City Council. These sites are *Ebonytown* in the middle of the Negro section; *Blendtown* on the "fringe" area near the Negro college; and *Voltshill* in the middle of what is now an all-white neighborhood. Choice must be made among these sites. The more militant Negroes do not want the project in the all-Negro section, rejecting this on the grounds that this kind of project is "Negro removal." Some of the leaders of SNRC own property in this area and they could conceivably benefit financially if the project were located in this area. The project in the fringe area would be more acceptable to these Negroes. There might be some opposition from the whites in the community (depending on where the project is located—if it is near Duke this might mean some conflict among the members of the Duke community). The same or more militant opposition will be found from those in the all-white area. Implicit in site selection is the problem of relocation. Who will be relocated? How? Since the Federal government requires that citizen participation be part of any urban redevelopment project, there will be opportunity for all groups to be involved.

In addition to site selection, a decision must be made as to the type of project. Urban redevelopment includes slum clearance, redevelopment, and conservation. Should both middle-income (to include the growing Negro middle class and the white-collar workers from the new industries) and low-income housing be included? Who should sponsor the housing—private developers (backed by both the Negro and white economic elites), or the government, or the union? The union has talked of sponsoring a low-income project which will not be as cheap as present housing, nor as expensive as privately sponsored middle-income housing. In order to do this, however, there might be a dispute within the Central Labor Council between white liberal labor and conservative labor over whether the project should be segregated or not.

There is, of course, the question of who would bear the burden of the taxes.

DESCRIPTION OF DURHAM

I. HISTORY OF DURHAM

Durham is relatively new as cities go—having developed from a railway station in an area of small farms in 1853 to a city of about 60,000 inhabitants in 1960. At the end of the Civil War, the Durham tobacco industry developed after Northern troops spread Durham bright-leaf tobacco across the nation.

A number of tobacco companies were formed in Durham to capitalize on the tobacco boom. In 1878, a tobacco company was formed there by Washington Duke and his sons along with George W. Watts. The Duke company turned to cigarette production to avoid direct competition with the pipe- and cigar-tobacco producers. Through mechanization and the driving force of James Buchanan Duke, the company quickly assembled a tobacco monopoly in the United States. The trust was dissolved by Supreme Court order in 1911, but not before J. B. Duke and others became fabulously wealthy. The tobacco men invested in other industries in Durham: George W. Watts and Benjamin Duke established Erwin Hosiery Mills; W. A. Wright founded a machine company; General Julian S. Carr invested in textiles, etc.; and J. B. Duke established Duke Power Company.

The social-cultural atmosphere of Durham also was shaped by tobacco money. In 1892, Trinity College was moved to Durham through the patronage of Washington Duke and Julian Carr; and in 1924, J. B. Duke endowed the college with $40,000,000 in return for the college being renamed Duke University. George W. Watts built and endowed a·community hospital, and he and others also aided the building and financing of Lincoln Hospital and North Carolina College (both Negro).

The political affairs of Durham were largely dominated by the white conservatives until the end of World War II. W. F. Carr, an executive of Durham Hosiery Mills, who had served on the City Council from 1917 to 1933, and as Mayor from 1933 to 1949, typified this ascendency. After the war, however, the influence of liberals and of the Negro community began to be felt. Much of this influence was due to the organization of the Durham Committee on Negro Affairs (DCNA).

II. DEMOGRAPHIC DATA

Unlike northern United States industrial cities, nearly every area in Durham has some Negroes. However, 6 census tracts are over 90 per cent Negro. Except for the Duke University area (tract 15), income, occupation, and age characteristics follow the white-Negro patterns. The Negro areas have generally the lowest average incomes, higher percentages in the lower occupational levels, and the youngest median age. Table 1 shows the census tract breakdown on these characteristics, and Figure 1 shows the correspondence between census tracts and wards.

III. PHYSICAL CHARACTER

Land development inside the city is relatively compact. The heaviest industrial and commercial development has taken place on the ridge along the Southern Railway which bisects the city from west-northwest to east-southeast. From this industrial and commercial corridor, residential development has spread almost equally to the north and south, with a larger proportion of the population residing north of the railway than south.

The Central Business District lies immediately to the north of the Southern Railway and is very compactly developed. This is due largely to the fact that it is almost completely encircled by industry and railroads. Commercial development extends out along the major streets radiating from the core. Two other smaller business centers have grown up in the east and west sectors of town as part of the industrial-commercial corridor. Three major shopping centers were established in 1959 and 1960, each about 2 miles out from the Central Business District. Industry has spread out from the central corridor in

TABLE 1

Census tract	Median age	Median income		Population by %		Total population	Median no. yrs. of school		Negro occupation: % in each class				General occupation: % in each class			
		Negro	General Pop.	White	Negro		Negro	General Pop.	I	II	III	IV	I	II	III	IV
1	30.8	-	6,378	99.2	0.8	6,532	-	12.1	-	-	-	-	31.0	23.8	21.3	23.9
2	35.5	-	5,354	98.4	1.6	2,854	-	12.1	-	-	-	-	41.8	20.7	17.2	20.3
3A	27.5	2,316	3,562	57.0	43.0	3,302	7.5	10.6	7.4	4.7	5.4	82.5	22.8	15.7	13.5	48.0
3B	34.5	-	5,810	98.3	1.7	3,725	-	12.9	-	-	-	-	47.6	22.5	13.9	16.0
4A	31.2	-	6,023	99.97	.03	3,622	-	12.5	-	-	-	-	48.5	17.1	17.1	17.3
4B	29.6	-	4,048	82.5	17.5	3,872	6.4	8.5	12.4	4.1	16.5	67.0	18.0	14.3	28.5	39.2
5	29.4	2,369	3,292	46.3	53.7	5,396	6.8	8.4	2.5	6.0	14.0	77.5	13.7	13.1	19.3	53.9
6	30.7	-	6,167	99.94	.06	3,285	-	12.7	-	-	-	-	54.8	15.6	14.1	15.5
7	34.0	-	5,212	88.8	11.2	3,771	5.6	12.3	4.5	4.5	14.5	76.5	40.8	19.1	12.8	27.3
8	34.1	-	3,038	78.4	21.6	1,952	6.2	9.3	18.5	0	6.2	75.3	25.7	11.0	25.7	37.6
9	25.6	2,552	2,701	6.7	93.3	3,473	7.2	7.4	3.2	5.6	14.3	76.9	4.7	6.2	16.0	73.1
10A	31.0	-	3,854	98.1	1.9	5,158	-	8.2	-	-	-	-	12.5	17.6	27.5	42.4
10B	28.6	-	5,777	96.3	3.7	3,423	-	10.2	-	-	-	-	19.5	22.0	27.2	31.1
11	32.1	1,577	2,940	82.4	17.6	4,387	6.5	7.0	0	4.7	33.7	61.6	4.9	10.8	31.5	52.9

12A	25.2	1,821	1,817	.03	99.97	3,381	6.6	6.6	3.1	3.5	11.1	82.3	3.1	3.5	11.1	82.3
12B	30.8	2,002	2,002	0	100.0	3,101	7.7	7.7	4.4	3.2	14.5	77.9	4.4	3.2	14.5	77.9
13A	27.1	2,534	2,534	0	100.0	2,690	7.9	7.9	10.8	5.7	10.4	73.1	10.8	5.7	10.4	73.1
13B	22.6	985	985	0	100.0	4,872	11.1	11.1	21.5	6.7	11.3	60.5	21.5	6.7	11.3	60.5
14	21.2	2,489	2,485	3.7	96.3	3,859	9.0	8.7	8.2	2.7	6.8	82.3	8.2	2.9	7.0	81.9
15	21.4	-	698	95.2	4.8	5,494	-	16.0	-	-	-	-	50.2	17.7	3.0	29.0
Durham	27.4	2,882	3,119	63.8	36.2	78,155	7.6	9.9	-	-	-	-				
Median Negro	24.8															
Median White	28.7															

COMMENTS

Occupation: Class I—professional; technical, and kindred workers; managers; officials; proprietors

Class II—clerical and kindred workers; sales

Class III—craftsmen; foremen, and kindred

Class IV—operatives; domestics; service workers; laborers

Where cells are empty in Negro categories it indicates that there are less than 400 Negroes in the tract. Categories marked "general" include both white and Negro. Census tracts 13B and 15 should not be compared with other tracts because these two tracts are composed primarily of college students. Tract 13B includes the NCC students and 15 the Duke students.

143

recent years, and is principally located along the railroads and throughout the eastern part of the city.

Duke University holds large tracts of land in the western section of the city, a fact tending to restrict development in that direction.

Many of the older areas of the city, particularly in the east and south, are characterized by a mixture of residential and non-residential land uses. Most of the newer sections are more homogeneous in character. Although there is relatively little undeveloped land in the city, densities are low, with single-family detached and duplex houses

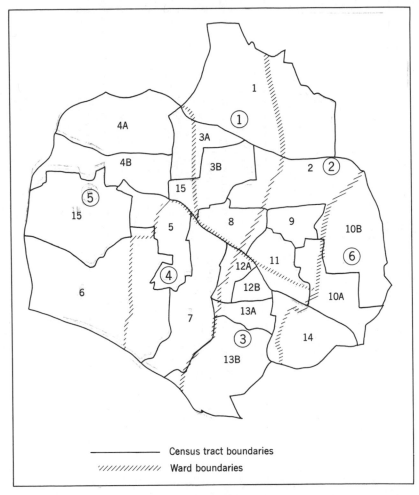

Figure 1. Correspondence between city of Durham census tracts and wards.

accounting for almost all residences. Although there are a few well-to-do sections, especially the area south of the Duke campus, the great majority of the houses in Durham are small, relatively inexpensive, and reflect modest levels of family income.

Like almost every industrial city, Durham has blighted areas. The largest of these areas are in the eastern and southern sections of the city, but the districts north and south of the Duke East Campus are also deteriorating. There are two officially designated redevelopment areas; the Hayti-Elizabeth area and the Central Business District.

The major street system in Durham is quite confusing. The railroad bisecting the city is partly to blame for the irregularity of connecting streets from north to south. As traffic continues to grow, the inadequacy of the circulation system may be expected to become the subject of more complaints. A circumferential expressway has been partially completed around the city. The uncompleted link is across the southern third of the city.

The topography of Durham is gently rolling hills.

Durham is physically unattractive for the most part. Commercial strips along the radial highways, rundown areas, miles of unpaved streets scattered throughout the city, and an ugly Central Business District all testify to the fact that the recently organized city beautification movement is sorely needed.

Further expansion of the built-up area is expected to be mainly toward the south, as a result of employment growth in the Research Triangle.

IV. ECONOMIC BASE

In the 1880's, Durham was the leading industrial city in North Carolina, tobacco and textiles being its chief products. The early history of the city sparkled with economic successes. Large landholdings around the city were developed by affluent private interests. These people were especially desirous of attracting new industrial capital. They offered to donate land for new factories, and they were willing to dispose of land in any manner the customer liked. Railroads followed new industry, and new tracks cut paths through many sections of the city.

The period 1945–1957 was a time of economic decline. Durham was not keeping pace with the rest of the state in industrial development. It was losing many of its wholesaling activities to other cities, and retail sales were declining. It was designated by the legislature as an area of chronic unemployment. Contributing causes were lack of community spirit, lack of leadership and imagination, poor physical organization of the city, and its unsightly appearance.

Developments since 1957 indicate a brighter economic future. The Research Triangle Area is a technical research center closely associated with major institutions of higher learning. The site contains 4,000 acres. There is a downtown urban renewal program under way. A downtown study on revitalizing the CBD is being undertaken. Thoughts revolve around a new government center, revised street system, parking, etc. There is an industrial park in South East Durham, which has been developed by local business interests. An east–west expressway is being planned as a federal urban aid project. A long-range recreation plan is sponsored by Durham County, Durham City, and voluntary agencies.

In 1960, industry in Durham occupied 951 acres and employed 6,300 persons in tobacco, 3,440 in textiles and 3,760 in miscellaneous industries.

Durham is the second largest manufacturing center in North Carolina. It has 124 industries including such diverse products as pipe tobacco, sheets and pillow cases, hosiery, flour, corrugated fiberboard containers, wooden boxes, medicines, lumber products, and roofing. It manufactures 19 per cent of the nation's cigarettes.

Durham has 6 hospitals, 4 hotels, Duke University, and North Carolina College. It has 3 commercial schools, 148 churches, 4 insurance companies (of which 2 are Negro), and is a terminal for air, bus, rail, and truck traffic.

V. FORMAL OFFICES (CITY GOVERNMENT)

A Council–City Manager form of government was adopted in 1921 and revised in 1947. Under the revised charter there are: A Manager; a Mayor, who presides over and votes with the Council; and a 12-man City Council with staggered 4-year terms for councilmen elected in at-large, nonpartisan elections. Three ward and 3 at-large councilmen are elected every 2 years at the same time as the Mayor whose term runs for 2 years.

The City Manager is the administrative head of the municipal government. He is empowered to appoint all subordinate officers of the city, with the exception of those appointed by the Council.

The Department of Finance is divided into 3 areas supervised by the Treasurer, the Auditor, and the City Tax Collector. These jobs are Council appointments. The Director of Finance is at the same time the City Manager.

The Planning Department is empowered to draft plans for city development and to recommend new projects affecting the public welfare. The director is appointed by the City Manager. The Planning and Zoning Commission holds public hearings on proposed zoning changes and makes recommendations to the City Council.

In addition, there are the usual departments associated with a city of this size: Police, fire, recreation, water, public works, and a board of education.

VI. GROWTH ISSUE

The growth of Durham is tied up with two major issues—urban renewal and annexation.

The goal of urban renewal is the improvement of 3 areas of the city: the Hayti–Elizabeth St. section, the Central Business District, and the area adjacent to North Carolina College. The Hayti area consists of Negro slums; 90 per cent of the homes are blighted and dilapidated. To deal with this, a 10-year program has been planned; it involves rehabilitation of those buildings that can be saved and clearance and redevelopment of the rest. Project 1, begun in May, 1963, will take 5 years. Clearance and relocation will take 2 years; water and sewage will be installed the third year; and 2 years will be devoted to selling the property to private enterprise. Project 2, taking place simultaneously with Project 1, will ultimately result in clearance of 24 acres of residential land, 14 acres of commercial land, and 3 acres of industrial land. The residential section is to be purchased by the Durham Public Housing Authority for construction of low-rent public housing. Four other projects will also be carried out.

The Hayti renewal program was recommended by a special study on planning. The City Manager disapproved it at first, but the Mayor and City Council supported it. The opposition was diffuse, consisting mainly of the radical right whose members disliked the program on ideological grounds (they saw it as being socialism and expansion of the federal government) and the slum landlords, who profited from the blighted properties. Nevertheless, a bond issue on the renewal program passed in the elections of 1963.

The urban renewal program has been supported by the Negro leaders as a benefit to the Negro community. Relocation has not encountered any organized opposition, probably because of the plans to construct public housing to cope with displaced families. Also the Negro councilman, Stewart, is involved in the redevelopment of the blighted area.

The downtown project grew out of a study made for the Downtown Redevelopment Association. The Mayor believed the city's future depended upon the revitalization of the Central Business District. City-owned parking facilities have been provided, and blighted buildings will be removed and street patterns planned for increased traffic.

Recently, the City Council unanimously approved a $16.1 million downtown rehabilitation program. The unanimous vote reflected the lack of opposition to the issue.

A program for the area around North Carolina College is also on the urban redevelopment agenda. This section consists of the better Negro residences, so that the emphasis will be on rehabilitation and improvement of existing structures rather than on clearance.

The second major growth issue is that of annexation. This proposal grew out of problems Hope Valley was having with its sewage. After the state directed Durham to look into the matter, the City Council gave the planners free range to draw up an annexation program of qualified surrounding districts. The City Council approved of the maximum plan submitted. Annexation will widen the tax base of the city and provide needed services to the annexed areas.

To ascertain the prospects for the annexation issue at the coming June referendum, we must examine the resistance to the unification proposal in 1961. Although unification of city and county had been supported by the City Council, most of the prominent city leaders, and the newspaper, it met solid defeat at the polls, with only 32 per cent of the city voting in favor of the proposal. Labor unions, taking their cue from the tax-minded tobacco companies and the Durham Committee on Negro Affairs, came out against unification.

Action has been taken to prevent these two blocs from opposing annexation. An agreement has been worked out with the tobacco companies so that tobacco storage warehouses will not be annexed. Also, the planners have included a Negro section in the proposed areas to be annexed.

Some opposition to annexation exists in the areas to be included, especially in upper-middle-class Hope Valley. But since the people in these areas cannot vote in the referendum, their opposition must be limited to appeals to the Durham electorate. If the Negro com-

munity does support the issue, as expected, the probability of annexation being defeated is minimized.

VII. OTHER ISSUES

A. Law Enforcement and Morals. The Durham police have been accused of negligence since the escape of 3 prisoners from the Durham Jail in August. Another issue concerns the so-called "piccolo" houses, vulgar magazines and books, and obscene movies. The police announced a crackdown on the "piccolo" houses. A Grand Jury requested the City Council and County Commissioners to consider the initiation of laws prohibiting the distribution of obscene materials.

There is divided opinion on a proposal by the County Sheriff to have a citizens' committee act as censors. A number of churches have circulated petitions supporting such a committee. The Durham Ministers' Association feels this censorship is the wrong approach, and vetoed the idea. The City Council has adopted a hands-off policy, with the City Attorney stating that state and federal laws are adequate.

B. A tax increase in 1965 was announced by City Council. The tax rate will be higher than that approved prior to adoption of the 1964-65 budget. The increase will be even higher if annexation is approved.

C. A proposal was brought before the City Council for a closed-cable television system. Fierce opposition has come from such business interests as movie houses and independent television repairmen. The opposition claimed that this would result in pay television. A study commission has been appointed by the City Council.

D. Recent zoning, limiting activities of automobile service firms, automobile graveyards, junk yards, and mobile home sales, met with opposition from groups affected.

VIII. NEGRO COMMUNITY

The Durham Negro community, sometimes called "the Negro business capital," is distinct from other Negro communities because of the nature of Negro businesses and economic interests. There are the usual Negro businesses (service establishments, barber shops), but there are also large Negro banking, real estate, insurance, savings and loan interests. As a result, the Negro leadership in Durham is basically capitalistic.

The North Carolina Mutual Life Insurance Company is the largest Negro-owned and Negro-operated business in the world. It has

assets of over $71,000,000 and has $291,000,000 of insurance in force. It is the largest home-owned firm in Durham, employing over 1,200 Negroes in some 50 different jobs. Asa Spaulding, the president, is well known in Durham, but does not play an active role in Durham politics.

A Negro bank, the Mechanics and Farmers Bank, has expanded to establish branches in Durham and elsewhere. Its president, John Wheeler, is influential in the Negro community, not only because of this position but also because of his position as head of the powerful Durham Committee on Negro Affairs.

A third leader in the Negro business community is John S. Stewart, President of the Savings and Loan Association. He has been on the City Council for 8 years, and is on friendly terms with the other members.

Financial interests and leaders appear to dominate the DCNA. The DCNA has become the principal channel for political communication between the races. On several occasions, its endorsements have spelled the difference between victory and defeat for a political candidate. Under its direction, the Negro community has been organized into a unified bloc vote. When the choice is between 2 white candidates, about 90 per cent of the Negro voters can be expected to cast their ballots for the endorsee; when a white candidate is running against a Negro, the latter may poll almost 100 per cent of the votes in the all-Negro precincts. The DCNA reaches its minimum strength when a Negro opposes another Negro. There have been 2 such contests. In both, the non-endorsed Negro candidate was J. T. Taylor, one of the founders of the DCNA, and a professor at North Carolina College; he ran against the endorsed Negro, J. S. Stewart, for the Third Ward seat in the election of 1957, and against R. N. Harris and a white candidate, M. T. Mangum, for the same office in the primary of 1953. In the Stewart-Taylor race, Stewart, backed by the DCNA, received 73.4 per cent of the vote in all-Negro precincts, 64.2 per cent in mixed precincts, 62.8 per cent in the predominantly white precincts, and 57.7 per cent in all-white precincts. The reliable strength of the organization with Negro voters is probably 60 to 70 per cent.

The size of the Negro vote in city elections also contributes to the maximization of Negro political influence. From 1951 to 1961, all-Negro precincts contained about ⅙ of the city's registered voters, and usually had a turnout rate higher than that of the rest of the city. Consequently, they usually cast a percentage of the total city

vote somewhat in excess of their proportion of registered voters. A Negro-white contest is associated with the highest vote totals, both of whites and of Negroes, though the pattern is more pronounced in the case of Negro voters. In a Negro-Negro contest, many whites consciously abstain from expressing a preference, thereby enhancing the ability of Negro voters to select, in effect, their own Negro councilman.

The important question is not the existence of a Negro bloc vote, but the DCNA's leadership of that bloc vote. The Political Committee of the DCNA interviews candidates and then presents its recommendations to the rank-and-file membership which, in theory, always retains the authority to alter the endorsement. In practice, however, it does not.

The mores of the white community have caused the DCNA to conduct Negro political affairs in a covert manner. The effect is to make the Negro community quite dependent on the DCNA for racial leadership in politics; this, in turn, relieves the mass of Negroes from any necessity to inform themselves about political affairs.

The Negro leadership has seemed to accept the idea that the Negro community is separate and segregated. Its goals seem to be the negative ones of protection from white repression, rather than the affirmative ones of integration of the Negro community into the broader community. McKissick, National Chairman of CORE, is co-chairman of the DCNA's economic committee. He is young, dynamic, and more militant than the older generation of Negro leaders. Thus far, however, there has been no overt struggle between McKissick and the older leaders.

There are, however, indications of an incipient split within the Negro community. David Stith, President of Southeastern Business College in Durham, plans to run against John Stewart in the Third Ward for the latter's seat on the City Council. Stith is dissatisfied with the level of services provided the Negro community. He feels that, if Stewart were less interested in his friendship with his colleagues on the City Council, and more of a battler for his constituents, the situation might be improved. The basic issue appears to be that the older leadership, after decades of dominance, is beginning to be challenged by younger and more militant elements. If Stith runs for the Third Ward seat, he will probably not receive DCNA support. If he decides to run for an at-large seat, he might be able to secure DCNA support. If the poorer Negroes are discontented with the DCNA, then the challenge might be a significant one.

ROLE DESCRIPTIONS AND ROOM ASSIGNMENTS

1. *Adams*. Chairman of SNRC; president of bank which includes branches both in and out of Durham; president, Southern Regional Council; member, Urban Renewal Commission, Committee on Community Relations; active in Democratic Party. Age: middle 50's.

Wields considerable influence in Durham, among whites as well as Negroes; somewhat moderate, although aware of pressures from the more militant Negroes and whites; opposed unification issue—hasn't stated position on annexation; pro urban renewal, although issue could bring about conflict between his financial interests and interests of the Negro community.

Main headquarters: State Mutual Life Insurance Building.

2. *Bailey*. Executive Committee of SNRC; president, Savings and Loan Association; member of the City Council since 1957; previous chairman of SNRC; member of the Democratic Executive Committee; Executive Committee, local chapter NAACP. Age: middle 50's.

Like Adams, somewhat in favor of the *status quo*; uncommitted on annexation; pro urban renewal.

Main headquarters: State Mutual Life Insurance Building.

3. *Carson*. Executive Secretary SNRC; Professor of Science at Negro college. Appointed to SNRC by Adams. Age: early 50's.

Unsuccessful candidate for County Commissioner in 1962 when he had SNRC support; cross-pressured between loyalty to SNRC hierarchy and to liberal Negro students and faculty.

Main headquarters: State Mutual Life Insurance Building.

4. *Davis*. Chairman of SNRC Education Committee; Negro College employee. Age: middle 40's.

Main headquarters: State Mutual Life Insurance Building.

5. *Harriss*. National leader of national civil rights organization; co-chairman SNRC economic committee; member of NAACP. Age: early 40's.

Chief liaison between student groups and Negro and white leadership; somewhat obligated to SNRC leadership for financial support; more moderate on local than national civil rights issues; usually supports SNRC candidates and stands on issues; could be pressured by more militant Negroes.

Main headquarters: State Mutual Life Insurance Building.

6. *Jones*. Negro labor leader; employed by Industrial Educational School; Democrat. Age: late 40's.

Challenged SNRC leadership in 1963—did not support candidate.

Main headquarters: Pittsville Community.

7. *Smith*. President, South States Business College; candidate for City Council, opposing Bailey; president, Neighborhood Council #1. Age: middle 30's.

Militant on civil rights issue; opposing Bailey on grounds that the Negroes have not gotten enough; uncommitted on annexation and urban renewal.

Main headquarters: Smith Campaign Headquarters.

8. *Franklin.* President of Negro student body; native of Durham; political science major; member of civil rights movement. Age: 22.

Militant on civil rights issue; has, up to this time, complied with Harriss' strategy; might be willing to oppose SNRC if more militant action appears to be profitable.

Main headquarters: Pittsville Community.

9. *Fox.* Vice-Chairman, Neighborhood Council#1; insurance agent. Age: middle 30's.

Politically aware; dissatisfied with Negro "gains" in Durham; supports Smith in opposition to SNRC and Bailey.

Main headquarters: Pittsville Community.

10. *Bird.* Chairman, Neighborhood Council # 2; works in tobacco factory; mid-management. Age: late 20's.

Politically aware; also dissatisfied with current status of Negro "mass" in Durham; not necessarily aligned with Smith, but trying to get what he can; will oppose SNRC leadership if it seems profitable.

Main headquarters: Pittsville Community.

11. *Doe.* At-large candidate for Council; businessman—architect and real estate businessman. Age: middle 40's.

Economic conservative.

Main headquarters: Southland Department Store Building.

12. *Mayer.* Incumbent Mayor; running for re-election; partner in the accounting firm of Mayer and Morris; member of Board of Directors of 5 financial institutions; elected member of City Council in 1957; did not run for re-election in 1961; elected mayor in 1963. M.A., American University. Age: middle 40's.

Pro annexation, urban renewal; moderate on civil rights; set up Commission on Human Rights.

Main headquarters: City Hall.

13.*Mann.* Central Merchants' Association leader; owns lingerie shop; attended Durham schools. Age: early 50's.

Vaguely progressive—pro annexation and urban renewal; uncommitted on civil rights.

Main headquarters: National Bank Building.

14. *Worthington.* Chamber of Commerce leader; vice-president of tobacco company; migrated to Durham from Brooklyn, where his father owns a haberdashery; M.A. in Business Administration from Harvard School of Business Administration; member, Rotary Club and Elks Club. Age: early 30's.

Speaks for tobacco and textiles; pro annexation if it doesn't include tobacco warehouses; pro urban renewal; uncommitted on civil rights.

Main headquarters: National Bank Building.

153

15. *Lander.* Board of Realtors spokesman; native of Durham; attended Duke University; partner in Lander and Brock Realty Company. Age: late 50's.

Pro annexation, urban renewal; uncommitted on civil rights.
Main headquarters: National Bank Building.

16. *Arrow.* Chairman of Citizens Committee for the Annexation Bond; former Councilman; member, President's Commission on Civil Rights; head of local radio station. Age: middle 50's.

Pro development, annexation, civil rights.
Main headquarters: National Bank Building.

17. *Wright, Sr.* Executive of local bank; active in state politics; masterminded successful Democratic gubernatorial candidate; has daily working relations with Adams and Bailey; his own financial interests include textile, insurance, banking and transportation; these interests make him a target for suspicion by whites who are anti-growth. The Wrights, Sr. and Jr., are closely identified with the current white Establishment consensus; they represent "planned growth," and are community progressive conservatives. Wright, Sr., does not live in the city or the county now.

Wright, Jr. While identified, like his father, as a "progressive," the son is much more affable; speaks freely, has a well-known point of view, considers himself pro-civil rights. He has been particularly identified with promoting the nearby Industrial Park, in line with modern "growth" ideology.
Main headquarters: National Bank Building.

18. *Mrs. Perry.* Second ward representative on Council since 1952; lawyer; not up for re-election; elderly.

Owns property in central and near central city; involved in redevelopment planning and administration; pro planning, annexation; moderate on civil rights.
Main headquarters: National Bank Building.

19. *Mrs. Rogers.* Descendant of old tobacco family; on Board of Trustees of Duke University; middleaged; married to physician; wealthy; has commitment to community welfare, especially education.

Pro annexation, redevelopment; moderate on civil rights.
Main headquarters: National Bank Building.

20. *Nelson.* Councilman at-large; savings and loan auditor; past president of Lions Club; president of Durham Chapter of the American Heart Fund. Age: early 60's.

Represents financial interests on the Council; good relations with Negro leadership.

Pro annexation, urban renewal; moderate on civil rights.
Main headquarters: National Bank Building.

21. *Caldwell.* City Manager; came here in 1963 from Winston-Salem; technician and an administrator; sensitive to politics of his position, but gets involved as little as possible. Age: late 30's.

Pro annexation, urban renewal.

Main headquarters: City Hall.

22. *Rivers.* City Planner; has been fortunate in having support and blessing of the manifest leadership for the projects he initiates; is identified with the Wrights, but also is heeded with respect by the City Council, Chamber of Commerce, and Merchants.

Main headquarters: City Hall.

23. *Smart.* Duke staff member; M.A. in Administration from the Maxwell School at Syracuse University; member of the Inner-University Committee on Higher Education. Age: middle 50's.

Pro annexation, urban renewal, civil rights.

Main headquarters: University Heights.

Bright. Duke faculty member; Ph.D., Yale; has written several books on local politics; member ADA and Duke Faculty Council. Age: 40.

Pro annexation, urban renewal, civil rights.

Main headquarters: University Heights.

24. *Workman.* Secretary, Central Labor Union; regional organizer for AFL-CIO Committee on Political Education (COPE). Age: late 40's.

Represents national labor viewpoint; was a leader of the defunct Negro-Liberal-Labor alliance of the mid-1950's; influence now somewhat dubious; therefore, cautious about taking a strong position against the White Citizens Council leadership of the union locals.

Annexation not a salient issue; any position taken against annexation would reflect an effort to exert pressure on City Council to give in to demands of city employees; knows and likes Bailey personally, but feels Smith would do more for the Negroes and would be more sympathetic to labor.

Main headquarters: Shopsville Community.

25. *Campbell.* Incumbent member of City Council; up for re-election at large; A.B. degree in Economics from UNC; Teacher's Certificate in Education; owner and proprietor of a sandwich shop; has served as a member of Durham County Board of Elections; currently a member of the executive committee of the Democratic Party. Age: late 40's.

Represents business and labor groups; uncommitted on annexation and urban renewal; moderate on civil rights.

Main headquarters: Southland Department Store Building.

26. *Chase.* Incumbent member of City Council, up for re-election—Fourth Ward; contractor; appointed to fill unexpired term in 1963; no previous political career; member, Associated General Contractors; Board of Directors YMCA; chairman of Board, Elks Club. Age: late 40's.

Rather politically naive; more in touch with civic organizations and good government groups than political groups; pro annexation, urban renewal; moderate on civil rights.

Main headquarters: Southland Department Store Building.

27. *Rice.* Sociologist at University; candidate for Council—Fifth Ward; precinct chairman, member of the county Democratic executive committee; member of the Central Council on Community Relations. Age: middle 40's.

Pro annexation, urban renewal, civil rights.

Main headquarters: University Heights.

28. *Murphy.* Incumbent member of the City Council—Fourth Ward; realtor; A.B., Duke University; member Elks Club, American Legion, Junior Chamber of Commerce. Age: late 30's.

Gut liberal; votes liberal point of view; pro civil rights, annexation, urban renewal.

Main headquarters: National Bank Building.

29. *Wilson.* Writer—frequent contributor to newspaper; lives in suburb under consideration for annexation; Ivy League educated; generally at odds with the City Hall Establishment; articulate; shuns alliances; personally opposed to annexation; not publicly involved in other city issues.

Main headquarters: Southland Department Store Building.

30. *Murdock.* Chairman, White Citizens' Council; running for Council against Chase, Ward 1; tobacco company employee; served as Sixth District Chairman of the Wallace-for-President Party in 1964. Age: middle 50's.

Pro segregation; urban renewal and annexation stands not known.

Main headquarters: White Citizens Council Headquarters.

31. *Zimmerman.* President of student body, Duke University; Duke is politically inactive, but it is assumed that events between 1965 and 1969 will activate that reservoir of manpower. Zimmerman is drafted and later returns to Law School, thus, is on the scene in 1969. He then sees the possibility of furthering a political career by rallying the community conservationist sentiment among University fraternities and other students. Perhaps has more experience or legitimacy than Wesley.

Main headquarters: University Heights.

32. *Brzezinski.* An unheralded labor organizer in 1965, this actor yearns for a return to the peak of the Negro-labor coalition of preceding decade. He sees this as "the wave of the future" and as both a road to greater legitimacy for the labor movement, and a bid to make Durham a showplace for nation-

al AFL-CIO political ideology. A new electronics plant brought to town between 1965 and 1969 has an active union tradition, which Brzezinski seizes upon; resident white union members are politicized to support the Great Society, and to accept the fact that Negroes also happen to be interested in the Great Society, so the coalition is reinstituted on a firmer foundation than previously. White labor learns to use its voting power to its own satisfaction, and no longer is envious or hostile toward the Negro bloc vote.

Main headquarters: Shopsville Community.

33. *Sloan.* White Citizens' Council Chairman, quiescent in 1965; the issues are not salient enough for Sloan to command attention for segregation. However, the events of DCNA strife make the White Citizens' Council realize that if they do not vote for Bailey, Smith will win. This traumatic turn of events whips the WCC into frenzy of electoral and other activity in 1969. Fewer in number, but more intense in position, Sloan's organization works against all desegregationists among whites, while trying to avoid entanglement in Negro politics. Seeks aid from outside forces.

Main headquarters: White Citizens' Council Headquarters.

34-37. Description of these actors written in Rules of the Game. They are the electorate who will actually simulate the election.

Main headquarters: Precincts 1 through 22.

38. *Baldwin.* Previously committed to SNRC, Baldwin's job with Adams' bank made him a middleman in bloc vote. In 1969, Baldwin is amenable to overtures from the dissident Negroes' political strategy. Has recently bought his own home, in a pleasant, but segregated area. Age: early 30's. NCC graduate, army veteran; has 3 children in public school.

Main headquarters: Pittsville Community.

39. *Tanner.* Negro leader; a shop steward in new textile plant; involved in union politics, proud of former SNRC strategy. Tanner is open to new strategies by Negro dissidents, and also of labor-Negro coalition attempt.

Main headquarters: Pittsville Community.

40. *Biggs.* Unemployed Negro, frequent character around Fox's precinct (Neighborhood Council #1); he has been unable to hold a job permanently, but has never been "on the road." He is an opinion leader who "holds out" in a candy store.

Main headquarters: Pittsville Community.

41. *Wesley.* The president of the Duke student body, from Atlanta; while he cannot vote, he mobilized students to do ward and precinct work in the 1968 national election, and those same political amateurs, eager to taste the dust of battle again, are ready to mobilize on behalf of a candidate, an organization, a cause, or a faction, according to Wesley's endorsement.

Main headquarters: University Heights.

157

42. *Green.* Assistant to the Registrar of Duke University; lives in a middle-class housing area in Fifth Ward; disapproves of the image of Duke as a "hotbed of liberalism" and decides to let it be known that there is another sentiment present among Duke employees; he is a Duke graduate, has the ear of the Business Manager, if not his sympathy. Desire is to see his hometown remain harmonious and dignified, and to have his *alma mater* keep out of the political headlines.

Main headquarters: University Heights.

43. *City Editor.* Served on paper only couple of years; belongs to no civic organization, thus his participation in community affairs is probably limited to reporting and interpreting news. Writes Sunday column on city affairs, but no personal opinion given; pro growth stand; favors urban renewal, annexation, beautification; opinion of SNRC is unfavorable; dislikes bloc vote; felt some Negro leaders had chip-on-the-shoulder attitude.

Main headquarters: The Durham Press.

9

THE PROCEDURES AND
USES OF SIMULATION

In the design of a simulation exercise, one of the first questions to be dealt with must be the *purpose* of the exercise. The purpose, in turn, will have a direct bearing on the *structure* of the exercise. In the course of designing games, we have come to realize that not all the potentialities of simulation can be realized in a single game. If some of these potentialities are to be stressed in a game, others must necessarily be down graded. If a designer wants an exercise that will effectively recreate the excitement and uncertainties of the political world for students or trainees, he is likely to use complex games similar to those constructed at the University of North Carolina. If he wants to encourage participants to think soberly and carefully about policy alternatives, he may wish to reduce the intensity and immediacy of the situation in which players make their decisions, and allow time for cool calculation and the scrutiny of options. If the designer hopes to use simulation to generate new data about human behavior in contexts that resemble real world relationships, he will wish to simplify his game and control as many variables as possible. Simplicity and the use of controls will enable him to re-run his game and discover which of the players' reactions are stable products of the situation and which are statistically insignificant occurrences. Finally, if the designer wants to build a simulate that will incorporate certain assumptions in order to explore the implications of those assumptions when the game is played out, he may wish to consider the use of computer simulation. Only by using a machine can he completely elim-

inate the distorting effect of player's personality on the model he has
built.

In addition to the broad decisions the designer must make in order
to relate the structure of a game to his purposes, is the determination
of the *degree of abstraction* to be used in connection with each major
element in the simulate. He might, for example, wish to simulate the
budgetary process in considerable detail, while doing relatively little
with the broader political process. If the experimenter chooses to use
a low level of abstraction and to incorporate a good deal of detail,
his simulate will probably be realistic in appearance but will be hard
to generalize from because it is so concrete and detailed. A more abstract simulate, on the other hand, will incorporate a certain amount
of distortion because so much is left out. It is likely to seem "unrealistic," but will probably prove easier to generalize from. Since the
complexity of a simulate increases sharply as more detail is added,
the decision concerning the degree of abstraction should be adjusted
to the capability of the players and the extent to which they will be
socialized into the game. If players have time to become acquainted
with a game, they can cope with a high degree of complexity. If they
lack socialization into the game, a relatively low level of complexity
may prove baffling.

The designer must decide on the *time scale* to be used. Simulation
can slow down fast processes or, as in the cases described in this volume, speed up slow processes. If the designer is interested in simulating relatively short-term processes of change, the ratio of real time
to game time would be low, and might even be 1 to 1. If he wants to
simulate the shifts of political coalitions over a period of several years,
however, then a higher ratio should be used. If the experimenter is
concerned with broad social change extending over a period of 8 or
10 years, the ratio of real time to game time would have to be very
high. If game time is to represent a number of years of real time, the
designer may have to allow for a number of changes in technology,
attitudes, and so on, that would normally take place over that span of
time. Instead of analyzing and miniaturizing an existing situation,
that is, the designer will have to attempt to approximate developments that are to take place in the future. This problem does not arise
if the game is designed to operate over a short span of real time.

The higher the ratio, the greater will be the disparity between the
time compressibility of the various activities that are to be incorporated. In an earlier chapter, it was pointed out that public meetings
and legislative sessions are not readily compressible. In a simulate

dealing with activities of these kinds, the designers should be modest in their conversion of game time into real time, unless they have found functional equivalents for the processes that are relatively non-compressible. It is difficult to provide guidelines for time scaling; a good deal will depend on the tempo experimenter wishes the exercise to have. If he wants to slow down the pace, an hour of game time can be made to represent a short span of real time. The tempo of events will also be influenced, of course, by the number of activities the experimenter includes in a given time span.

When the designer telescopes time, he necessarily introduces an element of distortion into his simulate. How great the distortion might be would depend on the design of the simulate, on the importance of time to developments in the field situation, on the amount of time that is to elapse, and on the extent of the telescoping. In the simulation of a negotiating situation, for example, players will have less time to deliberate than will the actors in the field situation. If the negotiation were normally conducted at a leisurely pace over a period of months, then it could probably be telescoped greatly without much loss of substance. If it were telescoped beyond a certain point, however, the amount of distortion would increase, players would suffer from overload, and their behavior would be modified.

Next, in the construction of a simulation exercise, the designers must decide on the *features* of the field situation to incorporate into the simulate. Decisions here will be heavily influenced by prior decisions concerning purpose, scope, desired degree of abstraction, and time scale. Within the framework established by these factors, the features selected for incorporation will be those deemed by the experimenter to be of central importance to the process under study. Which factors are deemed important will depend on the purposes of the designer and his understanding of the processes to be simulated.

As with other techniques of research, there is room for error at any point. The designer might mistakenly devote his attention to features of the field situation that are quite peripheral. However, if the designer is skillful, and if he carefully checks the simulate against the field situation from time to time, the likelihood of gross error is minimized. In addition, there is a final check when the simulate is used. If the exercise should produce results which are thoroughly out of keeping with the field situation, the designer would doubtless be moved to re-examine the construction of the simulate.

Next, the designer must decide two interrelated questions: Will players be given single or multiple roles, and will groups be monolithic or splinterable? In the Simuland exercise, each player had a single role. He was a member of the landed aristocracy, or he was a member of a military elite, and that was all. In subsequent games, however, players were given multiple roles. This is one of the major features distinguishing the exercises described in this book, from other experiments with man simulation. This innovation makes individual behavior far more rich, varied, and realistic, and also points the way to a more realistic treatment of groups.

In the Simuland exercise, once again, no provision was made for an individual who might wish to sever relations with the group to which he was attached. Groups were monolithic. There might be shifting coalitions among groups, but the groups themselves were indissoluble units. When this feature is incorporated into the simulate, the designer is saying, in effect, that the groups in the field situation are composed of individuals who are totally committed, and who are impervious to any cross pressures. As a practical matter, this is rarely the case, however. This assumption might be appropriate for teaching purposes, but it could scarcely be justified in a simulate designed for research. Individuals normally have multiple roles, and are torn and pulled by cross pressures. They also normally alter their group affiliations in response to changing loyalties. If players are to be given multiple roles, it is almost essential that groups be allowed to splinter. A designer will find that the combination of multiple roles for players and the splinterability of groups will add entirely new dimensions to man simulation.

If the designer chooses to introduce multiple roles for his players, this option has certain implications for the design of the exercise. The number of sub-games to be incorporated must be tied in with the number of roles the players are expected to play. A player cannot have more roles than there are sub-games in the exercise. Unless there is an articulated framework in which he can operate, unless he has resources at his disposal, and unless others are involved in a sub-game and care about its outcome, a player cannot really play a role. During the course of an exercise a player might decide that he was going to play the role of a stock market wizard or a sports car devotee or a philanthropist, but these efforts on his part would be irrelevant to the game (except insofar as his idiosyncratic behavior might provide distraction), since there would be no sub-game that would give these roles meaning. It should probably be noted that a small amount of distortion is necessarily introduced into the simulate because family and other roles are overlooked in favor of political and economic roles.

Next, the designer must make plans for the insertion of players into the game by the assignment of roles. The exercises described in this book differ in certain important respects from role playing as normally used in the social sciences. As a rule, a player is placed in a static situation and is expected to elaborate a single response to this situation. In the simulation exercises described here, on the other hand, the individual is placed in a situation that is changing all the time. A player cannot adopt a single mind set and adhere to it; he must adapt to changing circumstances.

By definition, man simulation revolves around role playing. In an exercise designed primarily for teaching purposes, the skill with which roles are played is normally not a critical factor. An exercise may still be a successful teaching device even if some role playing is erratic. If the experimenters are interested in using the simulate as a research instrument, however, the caliber of the role playing is important. Unfortunately, there are a number of problems in connection with role playing; though these difficulties should not be exaggerated, they should not be overlooked either.

For example, when individuals are placed together in a social situation and are allowed to communicate, they begin to respond as a group to certain things. Changes of mood may sweep through the players in a way that cannot be anticipated and that cannot be duplicated in successive runs of the game. Thus, although the players may be the same in repeated runs, they may behave in quite different ways. If a group of players should come to feel that they are out of things, they may become disgruntled and may, to a certain extent, withdraw from the game.

Distortion may be introduced by the very fact that the exercise involves simulation. The motivation of the players may be altered because they feel they are only "playing a game." This may make them more competitive or adventurous than they normally are, or it may change their behavior in other ways. While this factor needs to be weighed, it does not vitiate the idea of role playing in teaching situations. Players may be fully aware that they are involved in a game and yet become deeply immersed in it. The phenomenon is common. A competitor in an athletic contest who, in the heat of battle, remarks to his team members that the outcome is not important since it is only a game, is courting disaster. Theater, the movies, and television provide daily demonstrations of the capacity of the public to become involved in make-believe situations. It is this capacity for compartment-alization of the mind, or suspension of disbelief, that makes soap opera so reliable a form of entertainment.

Involvement of a player does not, by itself, guarantee that a role will be played skillfully. A player may be passionately involved in a role and yet act neither the way the designer of the game intended nor the way an actor in the field situation would behave. There are a number of reasons for this discrepancy, the most prominent one being the impact of the player's personality on his conception of the role. A role may be given a flavor in the hands of one actor very different from that which it would be given in the hands of another. If a prescribed role is uncongenial, an actor may subtly alter it or, by playing it indifferently, sabotage it. We have discovered that a player can play a role that is mildly uncongenial and still put his heart into it; however, there appears to be an upper limit on how uncongenial a role can be and still call forth a real effort on the part of the player. Conservatives have played liberals, and liberals have played conservatives, but if the player's alienation from the role is too deep he may not be able to project himself sufficiently into the role to play it effectively. Therefore, if the designer is attempting anything more than a training exercise, he should probably give thought to typecasting his players to make certain that roles and players are compatible. Also, he will want to incorporate rewards and penalties to encourage players to adhere to assigned roles. Players have varying levels of ability and varying degrees of adaptability, and the experimenter may also want to make some allowance for these variations.

A further problem with role playing is that a player, with the best of will, may simply *not know how* to play an assigned role. This inability may be explained by a culture barrier. In two of the exercises described in this volume, Americans were asked to play Brazilian and Chilean roles. Observers familiar with Brazil and Chile remarked that the distortion in the playing of these roles was not great, but some distortion was inescapable. An interesting way to test the signiificance of a culture barrier would be to play an exercise of this kind using Americans, and to rerun it in Brazil or Chile using nationals of those countries.

There are more cultural barriers than national boundaries. Students who played the roles of members of the Negro community in Durham were also trying to cross a culture barrier. A barrier of another kind involves the field of competence of a player. In the exercises described here, professional politicians were played by non-politicians or, at best, by fledgling politicians. Latin American military leaders were played by students who had an imperfect understanding of the military politics of Latin America. The player portraying a Latin American General is not a General. If he has had any military experience at all, it was in the military services of the United States, and at a less exalted level than that of General. In addition, graduate and undergraduate students were asked to play the roles of Presidents, cabinet ministers, and party leaders even though, needless to say, they had never occupied any of these positions. Man simulation calls for players to project themselves into situations that are somewhat foreign to them and, therefore, almost always, requires players to journey across barriers of one kind or another.

Having dealt with the matters mentioned above, the designer must now try to understand the processes at work in the field situation and devise means by which those processes can be reproduced in miniature. He must try to devise and incorporate within the simulate substitute mechanisms that will have approximately the same consequences for the miniature system that the corresponding mechanism has for the full-scale system.

The substitute mechanism need not be a miniature of the larger mechanism. All that is required is that it will function in an approximately equivalent way. It might, in fact, be quite different both in its structure and in its mode of operation. For example, the Durham City Council almost always acts unanimously, as a consequence of an informal consultative process involving leaders on and off the Council. Accordingly, in *Durham, 1965–1969,* it was decided that the substance of the Council's operation might be better simulated if the Council members never met as a group. Whenever an ordinance or other action received the appropriate number of signatures of Council members, it was deemed to have been passed. This arrangement obviated the danger that the Council might become a real decision-making body during the game, which would introduce a distortion; it also overcame the difficulties associated with having the Council in session while other gaming activities were going on. This device allows the Council to play a role in the simulate that is equivalent to the one it plays in the field situation; even though its mode of operation in the simulate is quite different from that in the field situation. That is, the device is funtionally isomorphic though structurally quite different.

Taking another example from the Durham exercise, the designers wanted to build into the game 3 levels of political activity—leaders, sub-leaders, and a passive electorate. The problem was to make certain that the leaders and sub-leaders paid attention to the passive electorate and that the leaders also took care to retain the adherence of sub-leaders. The device used was giving the passive electorate a substantial number of votes to cast, thus encouraging the leaders to be solicitous of their wants. In addition, leaders were given only 1 vote to cast; sub-leaders, presumably in close touch with voters and capable of exerting direct influence on voting, were given 3 or 4 votes. Many devices have been used in this and other exercises to achieve correspondence between the simulate and the system simulated; some of these were nominating conventions, campaigns, coalitions, weighted voting, and so on—all aimed at functional rather than mechanical isomorphism.

A set of substitute mechanisms might also be fashioned to achieve functional isomorphism without psychological isomorphism. The behavior of players in a simulation exercise can be realistic without the thought processes of the players paralleling those of actors in the field situation. Sanctions built into the game might produce equivalent behavior, but on a thoroughly different psychological basis. If a simulation exercise does not attempt to simulate relevant psychological processes, this should be borne in mind; and care should be taken not to draw conclusions about human reactions on the basis of that exercise.

The design of a simulate necessarily incorporates a good many theoretical, often implicit, assumptions. The designer makes an assumption when he decides to incorporate one feature and omit another. He makes an assumption when he fails to incorporate something without even considering it (in that case, an unexamined assumption). When the designer groups players together in a room, he is saying, in effect, that the basis on which they are grouped is the most important single aspect of the field situation. If the designer allows full and free communication among players, he is saying, in effect, that the counterparts of those players in the field situation have equivalent ease of communication. One of the best ways to avoid error in the design of a simulate, or to discover error once it has crept in, is for the designers to be highly self-conscious about the assumptions that are made. To as great an extent as possible, assumptions should be made explicit; error is far harder to find when it rests on an implicit assumption.

Having designed and run a simulation exercise, the final task of the experimenter is to analyze the results. The society created in miniature is far more simple than the society being simulated, but its analysis, nevertheless, presents challenging problems. There is little point in simulating something if one cannot analyze what has happened in the simulate. At present, the capacity to analyze what has happened in a simulate is not great, and, therefore, needs to be improved. An exercise should be studied by observers belonging to a variety of disciplines, and having a variety of interests. Each team of observers might analyze a complex exercise from a somewhat different perspective. A variety of analytic devices must also be pressed into use; they include communications theory, role theory, organization theory, decision-making theory, and small-group analysis. Simulations of the kind described in this volume create miniature societies, and almost any observational or analytic technique that can be applied to the full-scale society can also be applied to the miniature version.

The discussion, thus far, may have left the impression that the design of a simulate is mechanical. It is not. Answers may come slowly for a time, and then come on with such a rush that the designer may be given the feeling that the design is shaping up, and is "right." His *feeling* that it is right, however, does not mean that it *is* right. There is room for error every step of the way. This becomes clear if the simulation cycle is broken down into its component parts.

The cycle begins with a field situation as given. The observer analyzes this situation and attempts to grasp its central features and its dynamics. On the basis of the understanding and insight he has achieved, be they great or small, he constructs a simulate. The simulate incorporates a variety of mechanisms that, hopefully, are functionally analogous to the leading features of the field situation. Provision is also made for players. Next, the simulation exercise is conducted, and the researcher observes it. On the basis of his perception of the exercises, he makes an anlysis and draws conclusions. There might well be a second and third cycle in which the observer, on the basis of his analysis and conclusions, would re-examine the field situation, modify and redesign the simulate, rerun it, re-analyze it, and draw a second set of conclusions. There is opportunity for error, therefore, in the way the observer perceives and analyzes the game situation, in the way he constructs the simulate, in the way players play the game, and in the way the observer analyzes the results of the exercise.

Having dealt with the design, playing, and analysis of man simulation exercises, something should be said about the uses to which these exercises can be put. Simulation can be used in three main ways: For teaching and training purposes; as an aid to policymaking; and as an aid to research and to theory development.

The teaching and training potential of man simulation is very great. Learning is not confined to the actual playing of the game, but can take place at every stage of the simulation sequence:

During the data collecting stage.
While the field situation is being analyzed.
While the exercise is being designed.
While the exercise is being run.
During the post-game analysis.

The design stage is important for learning, since the attention of the designers is necessarily directed toward questions involving theory. Because the psychological involvement of the players is so great during the actual playing of a game, that stage also provides a highly favorable setting for learning. Players who had little knowledge of Brazil, before the Brazilian exercise began, acquired a great deal of usable information before it was over. Stress should be laid on the "usable" nature of this information, because information is of value in a game only if it can be manipulated and can be put to work. In addition, the chances are that information acquired while the individual is under stress and is emotionally involved is likely to be internalized more fully than information acquired more casually. However, the most important payoff for players is not the acquisition of factual information but the achievement of insight into political and social processes of a number of kinds.

Simulation of the processes of the developing nations has important implications for those who make policy. Officials have found it difficult, and often impossible, to anticipate the consequences of an action they take in a developing country. The interlocked processes of social, political, and economic change are so complex that, even if they were understood, it would be difficult to carry analysis more than a step or two forward without the help of a special tool of some kind. The complexity of the system and the way the component parts interact make it impossible for the unaided mind to grasp what is happening. In addition, there is often a need for speed in making a decision. Policy makers may need to achieve rapid insight into a situation that has arisen or may soon arise in a developing country, and frequently there is little time for the leisurely processes of traditional scholarly analysis. Moreover, traditional scholarship may have little fio offer, regardless of the amount of time available. The problems to be dealt with are new problems and involve new types of analysis. "Experience" provides no guide if it is not relevant experience. On the other hand, to fall back on a trial-and-error method of settling questions relating to the developing countries is unacceptable, since it is slow, inefficient, and costly in both political and economic terms.

What is needed is a tool that will allow policy makers to try out different developmental strategies and analyze their results before committing themselves to one strategy or another. Policy makers need to have a way of generating synthetic experience to take the place of actual experience. They need something, for example, that will serve as the politico-economic equivalent of war gaming. Political gaming, as described in these chapters, holds promise of meeting that need. It permits the experimenter to trace out the implications of complex strategies, to enjoy vicarious "experience," to try out alternative strategies, and to do it quickly.

To turn now to the third use of simulation: Can it contribute to research in the social sciences? The answer is not the same for computer simulation as it is for man simulation, and the remarks here will be directed solely toward the latter. Whether or not man simulation is a "research tool" depends on how the term is conceived. Man simulation is not a precision tool in the sense that a laboratory experiment might be; however, if research is thought of as systematic effort to learn that which is not presently known, it qualifies.

Simulation is likely to be most useful in the study of a situation in which a number of elements are interacting in complex ways. Other research techniques allow the researcher to deal with a large number of variables, provided those variables involve only simple relationships; or to deal with complex relationships, provided only a few variables are involved. Simulation holds promise of allowing the researcher to handle a large number of variables and complex relationships. This means that the analysis of complex systems, and even of whole societies, is no longer ruled out.

One of the most difficult challenges faced by students of national development involves precisely the complexity of the subject. The mind balks at unaided efforts to manipulate imaginatively the processes of a developing country. Models, or simulates, help satisfy the observer's need to simplify and organize his perceptions about the central processes of the nation being observed. The larger and more complex is the system being studied, the greater is the need for a model, a working model, of that system. The use of a working model allows the researcher to concentrate his attention on a reduced number of variables and to set aside a good deal of the "noise" that might otherwise distract him. Because of observational difficulties and the problem of time, a researcher has difficulty watching the elements of a vast social system develop and change, but he *can* observe and manipulate the elements in his model. A working model, therefore, can often have important heuristic or exploratory value. Because relatively few variables are incorporated in a working model, they can be manipulated easily, and the researcher is enabled to make imaginative and bold assumptions.

A second factor favoring simulation as a technique is that it combines the advantages of the comparative approach to the study of political systems with the advantages of the wholistic approach. In using the comparative approach, social scientists, as well as natural scientists, focus on selected variables, and study their behavior in different cases. This entails dissolving each case, or each whole, into its constituent parts. The approach has proved invaluable, but it may lead the researcher to give too little thought to the problems of synthesis. In addition to breaking a system down and studying its parts, a system must be studied intact and functioning. We gain little by studying or comparing structures in different developing countries if we do not first ascertain whether or not the functions performed by those structures are comparable in the countries under study. Likewise, we gain little by studying the relationship of variable A to variable B if we do not understand the way this relationship is connected with the dominant processes in the society under study.

The situation is further complicated if we are dealing with change. To understand change, we must first grasp the sequence of the events that are changing; we must also be able to pinpoint the variables that played an important role in setting the events in motion. In other words, in the study of national development we are confronted by a social science question of long standing: Is it possible to make valid generalizations about variables apart from their context, or does the fact that the variables *are* being taken out of context vitiate those generalizations from the outset?

Simulation may also provide an investigator with some of the advantages of the case-study approach, since the design and playing of a "game" dealing with a particular country is, for all practical purposes, a case study. Simulation also provides the investigator with the advantages of the comparative approach, once he starts noting similarities and differences among simulates of several societies. Furthermore, an investigator who is trying to simulate a political system will find himself asking a range of questions central to the understanding of the society. Who are the actors? What resources do they wield? What actions do they take? What are the relations among selected actors? An investigator is more or less driven toward the central questions, questions that illuminate the structure *and* functioning of that system.

Simulation is also likely to be helpful when, for one reason or another, the elements involved in a situation cannot be dealt with experimentally. The field situations described in this volume are obviously of that kind. One may speak of "experimenting" with simulation, but, in the strict sense of the term, the use of human players rules out the conditions necessary for a true experiment. An experiment involves the creation of two situations, an experimental situation and a control, that are alike in all respects but one. This single element is then varied in the experimental situation, while being held constant in the other. If the procedure has been carefully adhered to, the difference in results between the two can be explained only in terms of the uncontrolled element. It is clear from this that as long as players are used, it would be extremely difficult to create an experimental situation. Furthermore, in the exercises described here, a great many variables were left uncontrolled. Because the exercise cannot be repeated under laboratory conditions, and because a number of variables are uncontrolled, a researcher should not expect to draw hard research conclusions from these exercises.

A simulation exercise should not be thought of in the context of laboratory experimentation, but rather in the framework of model building in the social sciences. A simulate is a model of a field situation, and simulation is one of the forms of model building from among which a researcher may choose. Other forms include computer models, mathematical models, formal written descriptions, and two-dimensional pictorial models. Simulation differs from some of these forms of model building in that the features of the field situation that are hypothesized as being important are built into a *working* model and the model is then set going. The value of a good working model, of this or any other kind, should not be minimized. It can have a revolutionary effect on research. The study of macro-economics, for example, scarcely existed before the Keynesian model became available.

Before a model can be used, of course, the congruence between the model and the situation modeled must be established. In the first instance, the data generated by a simulation exercise do not pertain to the field situation, but, rather, concern the artificial world of the simulate. How useful these data will be in learning about the field situation will depend on the degree of congruence between simulate and field. Correspondence, or isomorphism, is a matter of degree. A simulate can have a low or a high degree of congruence with the field situation, or it can fall somewhere in between. It could not be wholly isomorphic unless the field situation were reproduced in its entirety.

If the congruence is high, an observer might be able to observe repeated runs of the simulate, and make judgments about the possible range of outcomes in the field situation itself. *If* the features that have been abstracted from the field situation are, in fact, the key features of that situation, and *if* the experimenter had devised adequate substitute mechanisms, and *if*, further, the players played their roles reasonably well, *then* analysis of the simulate might tell the experimenter something about that which is being simulated.

One of the problems associated with simulation is the difficulty of determining the extent to which a simulate is, in fact, isomorphic. When an observer analyzes the outcome of a simulation exercise, it may be hard for him to tell whether a given feature of that outcome is determined by the basic dynamics of the field situation or derived from some stray and uncontrolled variable in the simulate. If an observer believes that a simulate is highly isomorphic, when it is not, he is likely to draw conclusions about the field situation that will be wide of the mark. The analogue construction process is complex, and it is easy for the unwary to deceive themselves. A researcher needs to determine the areas in which his simulate is or is not isomorphic, and he needs to determine the extent to which that isomorphism is usable. An observer might, for example, be able to suggest the basic pattern of politics that is emerging in a field situation on the basis of his analysis of repeated simulation runs. He ought to be cautious, however, in predicting the outcome of a particular event, such as an election. On the whole, it is not the discrete events that may take place in a series of simulation runs that should be used for prediction, but the broad, persistent patterns.

An objection to simulation, often raised, relates to the question of congruence. It is asserted that one cannot simulate a situation until one understands it, and if one understands it, in the first place, there is no need for simulation. The same sort of objection could be made to any model-building technique. If one fully understands the field situation, then there is no need for a model; and if one does not understand it one is incapable of building a model of the situation. The response is, of course, that one starts with a limited understanding of the field situation and builds a model that incorporates this limited understanding. By studying the model and examining its workings (if it is a working model) one may achieve insights which, when checked against the field situation, can be built into a second-generation model which will, in turn, lead to new insights.

It is necessary to be clear on the distinction between congruence, on the one hand, and abstraction, on the other. Congruence has to do with the *accuracy* with which a simulate reproduces a field situation; abstraction has to do with the *detail*, or lack of it, with which a situation is simulated:

		Congruence	
		High	*Low*
Abstraction	*High*	High congruence, high degree of abstraction	Low congruence, high degree of abstraction
	Low	High congruence, low degree of abstraction	Low congruence, low degree of abstraction

This matrix makes it clear that a simulate could be highly abstract (i.e., incorporate only a few functional equivalents of the field situation) and yet be highly congruent. A simulate could involve a low degree of abstraction (i.e., incorporate many features of the field situation) and, of course, have a high degree of congruence. In addition, a simulate could have a *low* degree of congruence, whether the level of abstraction was high or low.

The significance of a low level of congruence with a field situation depends upon the purposes to which a simulate is to be put. It would probably rule out the use of a simulate for research purposes. On the other hand, a relatively low level of congruence might be tolerable in a simulate designed for teaching purposes. Despite the imperfections of the exercises described in this book, and despite the varying degrees of the players' familiarity with the exercises, each game proved to be playable. In short, a high degree of congruence with the field situation is not a prerequisite for a successful game. This is obvious if we reflect that a simulate such as Simuland does not aspire to be isomorphic to *any* system and yet is eminently playable. The range in which political gaming will "work" is a broad one, therefore, and persons interested in the technique should not hesitate to try their hand.

Under certain circumstances, an exercise could be used both as a research tool and as a training device, but the experimenter should be alert for signs of incipient conflict. If an exercise is designed for teaching, the experimenter may wish to have it loosely structured so as to leave the players relatively free from constraint. In a game designed for research purposes, on the other hand, the experimenters may want a highly structured exercise that controls as many variables as possible. Again, for teaching purposes, it is important that each player has something to do all the time so that he does not feel left out of the game. If the designer tries to satisfy that condition, simply to keep player morale high, he may introduce a distortion. In a field situation there are times when actors are inactive and out of things. The designer will be tempted, therefore, for the convenience and happiness of his players, to introduce a distortion into the game. Even when an experimenter feels that he is being hard hearted, he may still be making concessions to player comfort and morale. The three roads (teaching and training, policy guidance, research and theory building) may parallel for a time; but when they part, the experimenter must be prepared to make his choice from among them.

If he chooses the research road he will find that simulation may provide a means for studying many matters that are impossible to study in a laboratory setting, and extremely difficult to study in society as a whole. To mention a few, these would include the following:

The impact of differential levels of information in a society.
The processes of ideological change and ideological conflict.
The intricacies of decision making.
The processes and psychology of negotiation and bargaining.
Political participation and alienation.
Morale.
Comparative leadership patterns.
Processes by which leadership emerges in comparatively unstructured situations.

The manner in which different sub-systems in a society mesh with one another.

The way in which individual actors adjust to role conflicts.

The way in which individuals adjust to various types of stress in social situations, including overload, and severe reduction of decision-making time.

The effect of differential perceptions by individuals of a shared situation.

In addition to these areas of research opportunity, the vast field of social change itself may be opened up by simulation. Not much is known about social change. If this seems a startling assertion, it is only because men tend to be more aware of what they know than what they do not know. A century ago social change was understood even less than at present, but this ignorance did not appear to men to be ignorance, since scarcely anyone conceived that it could be replaced by knowledge. It may be that men do not become conscious of an area of their ignorance until they are ready to try to overcome it.

Progress in the study of social change has been slow because men have not set themselves the task of understanding it; and they did not, because they lacked tools adequate to the task. Just as a number of fields of biological research could not emerge until the microscope was developed and the study of astronomy was severely limited until the telescope and spectroscope were developed, in the same way social analysis was for a long time cramped and confined. Recently, however, new tools and approaches, that may change all this, have begun to take shape. These include communications analysis, small-group studies, organization theory, systems analysis, and simulation.

These tools can, and should, be used in conjunction with one another. Simulation and systems analysis fit together very well, for example. Processes that are simulated can often be analyzed in systems terms. One of the features of simulation is that it is infinitely expandable. It is system-wide in its application, and if a social system is analyzable, it can be simulated, whatever its size. Simulation, therefore, can be used to study a sub-system within a society, the relations among sub-systems, the relation between sub-systems and the broader society itself, or the relation of a system to its environment. If a researcher wants to focus on the "political system," the systems approach helps him to remain aware that society is composed of a multitude of other systems and sub-systems to which the political system, through inputs and outputs, is directly and indirectly connected.

Simulation, along with the new analytic tools, opens large-scale social change to effective study for the first time. The exercises described in this volume simulated some of the processes of developing nations. Next, these and other processes should be simulated more fully, using a combination, perhaps, of man and machine simulation. Local political processes could be simulated along with national processes. Social structure, demographic factors, and changing attitudes ought to be incorporated into the simulate. Perhaps, by noting the key decisions that have been taken in a country over a period, then programming them for a computer, it might be possible to simulate the working of "tradition." A nation is more likely than not to continue to behave in accordance with its past conduct, and the influence of the past and of established attitudes could be simulated by the use of probability scales. There is no theoretical limit to the level of complexity that can be simulated. The limits are practical ones—the purpose of the exercise, the difficulty of its design, the availability of data, the relative importance given to human players and machines. In time, it should be possible to have an urban exercise within a national game within an inter-nation exercise.

The use of modular sub-games needs to be explored. Using the same basic simulate, it should be possible to develop for a given country a variety of sub-games that could be plugged into the main game or could be left out, depending upon the needs of the researcher. Sub-games dealing with public administration, community planning, local government, military politics, and economic planning, might be developed. This would have important training possibilities as well as research potential.

The development of a series of country simulates would open up a new technique for the comparative study of social, political, and economic systems. It should also help overcome an excessive concern with typicality in the study of the emerging areas. It may help observers to think in terms of typologies and multiple patterns of development rather than in terms of a single master pattern.

Simulation has only recently begun to be applied to social systems, and the technique is still in its infancy. In these circumstances, it is easy to project the technique into the future, and see it outrunning its present capabilities. Nevertheless, it is by forethought that investigators decide what is worth doing and what they should try to do. The limits of the approach must be probed, and harsh demands must be made of computer and man simulation. If rapid progress is to be made in the understanding of social change by means of simulation, new hands must be drawn into the work, minds must be kept flexible, and designers must stay chronically discontented with their efforts.